S0-BOJ-520

Folks are usually about as happy as
they make up their minds to be.

—Abraham Lincoln

MYSTERIES OF COBBLE HILL FARM

Digging Up Secrets
Hide and Seek

MYSTERIES OF COBBLE HILL FARM

Hide and Seek

BETH ADAMS

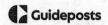

Mysteries of Cobble Hill Farm is a trademark of Guideposts.

Published by Guideposts
100 Reserve Road, Suite E200
Danbury, CT 06810
Guideposts.org

Copyright © 2024 by Guideposts. All rights reserved.

This book, or parts thereof, may not be reproduced, stored in a retrieval system, or transmitted in any form or by any means, electronic, mechanical, photocopying, recording, or otherwise, without the written permission of the publisher.

This is a work of fiction. While the setting of Mysteries of Cobble Hill Farm as presented in this series is fictional, the location of Yorkshire, England, exists, and some places and characters may be based on actual places and people whose identities have been used with permission or fictionalized to protect their privacy. Apart from the people, events, and locales that figure into the fiction narrative, all other names, characters, businesses, and events are the creation of the author's imagination and any resemblance to actual persons or events is coincidental.

Every attempt has been made to credit the sources of copyrighted material used in this book. If any such acknowledgment has been inadvertently omitted or miscredited, receipt of such information would be appreciated.

Scripture references are from the following sources: *The Holy Bible, King James Version* (KJV). *The Holy Bible, New International Version* (NIV). Copyright ©1973, 1978, 1984, 2011 by Biblica, Inc. Used by permission of Zondervan. All rights reserved worldwide. www.zondervan.com.

Cover and interior design by Müllerhaus
Cover illustration by Bob Kayganich at Illustration Online LLC.
Typeset by Aptara, Inc.

ISBN 978-1-961126-86-2 (hardcover)
ISBN 978-1-961251-43-4 (softcover)
ISBN 978-1-961126-87-9 (epub)

Printed and bound in the United States of America
10 9 8 7 6 5 4 3 2 1

MYSTERIES OF COBBLE HILL FARM

Hide and Seek

GLOSSARY OF UK TERMS

biscuits • cookies

bloke • man (informal)

charity shop • thrift store

cheese toastie • grilled cheese

football • soccer

had a monk on • angry or in a bad mood

wellies • Wellington boots

Ranks of British Nobility in Descending Order:

Duke

Marquess

Earl

Viscount

Baron

Baronet

CHAPTER ONE

Harriet Bailey slowed and steered the old Land Rover into the driveway. She bumped over the dirt and veered toward the entrance to Cobble Hill Vet Clinic, which was attached to the side of the house. Surrounded by lush gardens and sweeping views over the moors, the stately brick estate in the Yorkshire countryside had belonged to her grandfather, and Harriet still couldn't believe she got to live there now. The late Monday afternoon sunshine gilded the roses, delphinium, and foxglove in the garden, creating a riot of colors behind the low garden wall. She'd moved to England to take over her grandfather's veterinary practice, and it all still felt like a dream.

Harriet parked the Land Rover next to the clinic entrance. She paused to thank the Lord for bringing her to White Church Bay, as she had hundreds of times since her move. Then she hoisted her bag from the back, climbed out of the vehicle, and stepped inside the clinic. She smiled at the two people in the waiting area. She recognized the woman, and there was also a man she didn't know with a beautiful bloodhound at his feet. She didn't recall a bloodhound on the schedule today, so maybe he was a walk-in.

"How did it go?" Polly Thatcher asked from behind the receptionist's desk. In her midtwenties, Polly had gray eyes and dark hair, and had worked for Harriet's grandfather. Harriet didn't know where she'd be without her. Charlie, the calico office cat, perched on the counter.

"A strained ligament," Harriet said. "The horse needs to rest. No jumping for a month or so, and I left some other instructions as well." She stroked Charlie's head as she walked past.

"I bet Mr. Phillips didn't love that."

"I think he realized that, all things considered, a few weeks off is a pretty good outcome. It could have been much worse, even permanent. And he knows that if he pushes it, he's likely to be dealing with that," Harriet said. She loved animals of all kinds, and Helga the Hanoverian horse was beautiful and well-tempered. Helga had done well at horse shows, judging by the ribbons Mr. Phillips displayed along the back wall of the stable. "She should be fine as long as Mr. Phillips follows my instructions. And she's important to him, so I think he will."

"I'm glad to hear that." Polly beckoned to the man with the bloodhound. "Mr. Osbourne, if you'll follow me, I'll get you set up in a room."

The man who stood was probably in his midfifties, with salt-and-pepper hair and a black T-shirt over his dirty jeans. "Come on," he said to the bloodhound, and the dog obeyed and followed him toward the door Polly held open. Harriet noticed the dog wasn't on a leash. He didn't even have a collar, actually.

Polly closed the door behind them, and Harriet smiled at Sahaana Mehta. She had glasses and long dark hair threaded with gray, and she wore a baggy cardigan over her long, flowered sari.

"I'll be with you in a moment, Mrs. Mehta," Harriet said, stepping forward to pet the woman's black lab, Pitch. He licked her hand. "How's this guy doing?"

"Poorly," Sahaana said, her brow creased with concern. "He's been sick and sluggish lately. I think he ate something that disagrees with him."

"Well, we'll bring you back and get it worked out in a few minutes," Harriet promised. According to what Polly had told her, Pitch regularly ate things that made him sick. "We'll get him fixed up."

"Thank you." Sahaana patted the dog's head. "I appreciate it."

"It's what we're here for," Harriet said. She stepped through the door and into the rear of the clinic. Maxwell, the clinic's resident long-haired dachshund, rushed over to greet her, the wheels of his prosthesis squealing.

"Hey, buddy." Maxwell gazed up at her, his tail wagging as his tongue hung out, and she reached down to pet him.

"Mr. Osbourne is in Room Two," Polly said.

"Thank you," Harriet said. "What's the dog's name?"

"He doesn't know."

"What?"

"He'll explain." Polly pressed her lips together. "I'm pretty sure it's Coleridge though."

"Coleridge?"

Polly flapped a hand at her. "I'm getting ahead of myself. I'll let Mr. Osbourne tell you what's going on."

"Okay." Harriet didn't know what to make of the exchange, as it wasn't like Polly to be cryptic. But she stepped inside the exam room and smiled at the man who sat in the wooden chair kept for clients, the dog at his feet. "Good morning. I'm Dr. Bailey."

"Archie Osbourne." He stood and offered his hand to shake, even as he ducked his head shyly. "You're Old Doc Bailey's grand-daughter, is that right?"

Harriet shook his hand. "That's right. Did you know my grandfather?"

"Everybody knew him. He was a wonderful man."

"Thank you," Harriet said. "He really was one of a kind. I've got some big shoes to fill."

"We're glad you're here," Mr. Osbourne told her.

"And who's this?" Harriet bent down and held out her hand so the dog could sniff her and then stroked his head.

"I don't actually know," Mr. Osbourne said. "I'm a gardener, and I was working in Miss Birtwhistle's rose beds when this guy came wandering down the street."

There were several things that were surprising about this, not the least of which was the fact that Miss Jane Birtwhistle, a local cat lover Harriet had become acquainted with, had a gardener help her with her famous roses. But why would a dog like this be wandering the streets alone? If she was right in guessing that he was a purebred bloodhound, he was worth quite a bit. He was in good health, with no signs of contusions or dehydration. He couldn't have been on his own for too long, and he looked well cared for.

"He didn't have a collar, and there was no one with him," Mr. Osbourne continued. "I worried he was lost, so I brought him here to see if he had a microchip."

"That was good thinking," Harriet said. "Let's check it out." She opened a cabinet, took out the handheld scanner, and then reached for the loose skin on the dog's neck. The dog shifted his weight but otherwise didn't seem fazed as she felt along his skin. "I'm afraid I'm not feeling a chip."

"Oh dear," he said. "Well, I'm not really sure what to do with him, in that case."

"Hang on. Polly thought she recognized him. Let's see what she thinks." Harriet opened the door and called for Polly, who came quickly. "I didn't find a chip," Harriet said. "But you thought you recognized the dog, didn't you?"

"It's Coleridge," Polly said. "Liam Beresford's dog. He's been bringing Coleridge here since he was a puppy."

Harriet wasn't sure if she imagined the way Mr. Osbourne's eyes widened when he heard the name. She had never heard of Liam Beresford, but she was sure he would want his dog back.

"That makes it easy," Harriet said. "Why don't we call him and let him know we've got his dog here?"

"Sure thing," Polly said. "I'll do that now." She hurried away.

"Thank you for bringing him in," Harriet said to Mr. Osbourne. "I'm grateful you took the time to do it, and I think Mr. Beresford will be as well."

"I didn't want anything to happen to him," Mr. Osbourne said, scuffing the toe of his boot against the floor. "I feel sort of responsible for the dog until his owner's been notified."

They chatted for a few moments. Mr. Osbourne told Harriet how her grandfather, an esteemed artist as well as veterinarian, had taught his son to paint a decade before. Harriet loved hearing such stories about Grandad's influence on those around him.

Polly returned and poked her head into the exam room. "There was no answer at the Beresford place. I left a message."

"Does Liam have a cell phone?" Harriet asked.

"If he does, the number isn't in our records," Polly said. "So hopefully he'll return our call soon. I've put Mrs. Mehta in Room One."

"Guess I should get back to Miss Birtwhistle's roses," Mr. Osbourne said, gazing down at Coleridge. "Will you be all right, buddy?"

"He's safe here, Mr. Osbourne. We'll get him home," Harriet assured him.

"Thanks, Doc," he replied.

"No problem. I need to go check on Pitch. Polly, would you walk Mr. Osbourne out?"

Harriet walked to the other exam room and chatted with Sahaana while she examined Pitch. Sahaana had noticed something was off that morning when he didn't bound out the door and then refused to eat his breakfast.

"He was chewing on some crab shells down at the beach yesterday," Sahaana said. "So it could have been that. Then again, he was also nosing around in the garden, and he could have found anything there."

"I'll give you some antinausea pills, which will get him right back on his feet," Harriet said.

"Thank you." Sahaana peered up at Harriet through glasses that made her eyes appear larger than they were. "You know, I was worried when I heard how young you were. I thought there was no way someone in their early thirties could hold a candle to Old Doc Bailey, but you're every bit as good as he was."

"Thank you." Harriet smiled at the backhanded compliment. "My grandfather was a great man and a great veterinarian. So that means a lot."

A parade of dogs and cats and a pet parakeet kept Harriet busy, and when it was time to close late that afternoon, she found Coleridge behind the desk, next to Maxwell. The clinic's resident pup was delighted to have a friend, but Coleridge was pointedly ignoring the little dog. Charlie was perched on the counter, tail swishing back and forth.

"Did Coleridge's owner call?" Harriet asked Polly.

"Not yet," Polly said.

Harriet could board him in the kennels on the property if needed, but she would prefer to reunite the dog with his owner, who no doubt missed him. In fact, it was entirely possible that they hadn't heard from Mr. Beresford because he was out searching for Coleridge and hadn't been home to check his messages. "I assume we have Mr. Beresford's address in our records, right? Maybe I'll go drop Coleridge off."

"I bet he would appreciate that," Polly said. "And you should check his house out anyway. Your place here is really nice, but his is something else entirely."

"What do you mean?"

"It's the Beresford house," Polly said, as if that would mean something to Harriet.

"Yes," Harriet replied. "I assumed that was where Liam Beresford would live."

Polly shook her head. "No, it's Beresford Manor. As in, the home of Lord Beresford. The Baron Beresford, formally."

Why was she using his last name so much? "You mean, he's, like, royalty?"

"Not exactly." Polly laughed. "Sometimes I forget you're American, but then sometimes it's so hilariously obvious. He's a baron. That's a title of nobility. It's just below Viscount."

"Oh. Okay."

Polly looked like she was about to explain but then shook her head and said, "The point is, he lives at Beresford Manor, which is the house that accompanies the title. It passes down from one baron to the next, along with the money made from the land, to whoever inherits that title. The place is huge and old, literally from another time. And if you haven't seen it yet, you really should check it out. If you thought Ravenglen Manor was something, wait till you get a look at this place."

Ravenglen Manor was the estate of Julian Montcliff, who had recently been charged with insurance fraud by staging a jewel heist of his own collection decades ago.

"Where is it?" Harriet asked, wondering if she'd passed by it at some point without knowing it.

"Outside of town a little ways, to the north, opposite direction of Ravenglen Manor, and perched on top of a cliff. It's set back a bit, so you can't see it from town, but it's there."

"Can you get me the address?"

"Sure, but you won't need it. Just drive north from town until you get to the stop sign and turn right. You'll drive for a while before the road curves around some sheep in a field, past the old elm, and it's there. You can't miss it."

It sounded simple enough, but she still programmed the address listed in the clinic's computers into her phone. She'd learned that what seemed like simple directions to the people who'd grown up in White Church Bay didn't necessarily end up being simple to someone new to driving on the left side of the road.

She brought Charlie and Maxwell through the door to her house and filled their bowls, and then she led Coleridge out of the clinic and to the van. She'd been worried he wouldn't follow without a leash, but the dog walked behind her obediently. She opened the side door of the Land Rover and settled the dog inside, put the Beast in gear, looked both ways, and pulled out onto the road.

Cobble Hill Farm, the property her grandfather had called home, was a beautiful estate, holding not only the house Harriet had inherited and the veterinary practice, but the dower cottage and grounds that her aunt Jinny had inherited from her father and where she lived and saw patients as a general practitioner.

And just across the vet clinic's parking area sat the old outbuilding that Grandad had turned into his art studio and gallery. In his later years, he'd become known for his paintings nearly as much as his veterinary practice.

The low stone wall that separated the estate from the road was covered with spots of green lichen and bits of moss that only made it look more charming. Oaks and hawthorns arched over the roadway, and the neighboring houses quickly gave way to pastoral farmland as she drove north, away from the village of White Church Bay.

Harriet turned right at the stop sign and followed the curve, past woolly sheep grazing on the hills. Sure enough, a huge old elm tree, with a thick, knotty trunk and strong arms that spread a green canopy over the road, was just up ahead. She drove past the elm and kept going for a few miles before she came to a long driveway off to the right.

She'd been past the place a few times since she'd moved to White Church Bay but had never really noticed it. The property wasn't as easy to spot as Polly had promised. But once she turned into the driveway, she saw that it was lined on both sides with more elms and wound around a gently sloping hillside, past a pond, until eventually the house came into view. Coleridge began to thump his tail and howl when he saw the house. He knew he was home.

And what a home it was. She'd been expecting a big house, based on Polly's description, but this was on another level. The three-story manor was built in gold-colored stone with peaked gables on both sides of the facade and dozens of mullioned windows. Half a dozen stout chimneys rose from the roof, and a circular driveway fronted the house, which was surrounded by rolling green fields. Harriet could see formal gardens and several outbuildings beyond the house, and sweet peas and phlox and delphinium bloomed in the beds surrounding the driveway.

She parked in the section of the driveway that bowed a bit and stepped out uncertainly. There were two other cars there, a compact sedan with several dents and dings, and a sleek black Bentley. They looked incongruous, side by side, and her battered old Land Rover only added to the discord. She let Coleridge out and headed for the front entrance. The massive door—painted a dark blue and framed by a stone pediment, was imposing, which she supposed was probably the intent. There was a doorbell, so she pushed the button and waited. She didn't hear anything inside the house and had started to wonder if she should ring again when the door flew open and an older woman in jeans and a flowered top stood there, staring back at her.

"Oh. Hello," the woman said. As Coleridge pushed his way inside, she added, "Coleridge? Where have you been?"

"I'm Harriet Bailey," Harriet said to the woman, who looked thoroughly confused by what was happening. "I'm the new vet in town. I took over the practice from my grandfather, Harold Bailey." The woman nodded, but Harriet could tell it wasn't entirely registering.

"Someone found this dog in the village and brought him to me, hoping I could find the owner," Harriet continued. "Polly, who works with me, recognized him and said he lives here."

"He does indeed," the woman said. "But where's Lord Beresford?"

"Excuse me?"

"Lord Beresford. He wasn't with the dog?"

"No," Harriet said. "At least, not since I've had him."

"That's very strange," the woman said. She seemed to be in something of a daze.

"I assume that means he's not at home?" Harriet said. Coleridge sniffed about the foyer.

"Oh, yes. I'm sorry. This is all very confusing, but I—" She shook her head. "Please, come in." She gestured for Harriet to step inside and then closed the door behind her. They stood in a soaring hall, with black-and-white tile floors and a massive mahogany staircase that turned at a landing as it rose to the gallery along the second floor. The walls were paneled in matching mahogany, and portraits of men dressed in clothing from various periods of the past were hung in long rows. To the left and to the right, enormous doorways led to large rooms, which appeared to be filled with more artwork and antique furniture.

"I'm Mrs. Lewis," the woman said. The dog trotted off, clearly comfortable in this house. Harriet guessed he was looking for his owner. "I come here a few days a week to cook and clean for Lord Beresford. He's 'most always here, you see. He doesn't go out much, except to take Coleridge for walks, and if he has an appointment, I always know about it. But today when I came in, he wasn't here, and there's nothing in his diary about an appointment. He always writes his appointments in his diary."

"Perhaps he was called away unexpectedly?" Harriet hoped the words would soothe the woman, who seemed to be getting worked up, but Mrs. Lewis shook her head.

"The thing is, I don't think he's been here for several days. When I left Friday at noon, everything was fine. I had to pick up my grandson from school, you see. My daughter Marian was out of town for the weekend, a hen's trip with her school friends, and we got to keep little Grant, and we had so much fun with him. He's only five, and he's such a doll."

Just as Harriet was trying to figure out how to get her back on topic, she seemed to remember what she was saying. "Anyway, I left here around noon, and he didn't say anything about plans to go out, but when I showed up today, the mail had piled up, and so had the newspaper."

"No one else took it in?" Harriet asked.

Mrs. Lewis blinked and narrowed her eyes. "Who would have done so?"

"I'm sorry." Harriet could see she'd upset the woman. "I don't mean—I just thought, surely he doesn't live in this big house all alone?"

She nodded. "Lord Beresford is the only resident since his wife passed. There's no one else who would have collected the mail and the like. The gardeners and the men who deal with the estate don't come into the house. I'm the only one who works inside. Have been, since Beatrice passed."

Harriet assumed Beatrice was the baron's late wife.

"Well, maybe he decided to go away for the weekend?" she suggested. "A holiday, like your daughter?"

Mrs. Lewis narrowed her eyes, but then she shook her head. "You're new here, of course. The thing is, Lord Beresford doesn't really go on holiday. He doesn't like to leave the house much at all."

If Harriet lived in a place like this, she wouldn't want to leave it either.

"He's something of a recluse," Mrs. Lewis continued. "Aside from his walks along the cliffs with Coleridge, he pretty much doesn't leave. So for him to vanish like this is totally out of character."

"Have you tried calling him?"

"He doesn't have a cell phone," she said. "Old-fashioned that way. Well, in most ways. Says he doesn't need one because he never goes anywhere, which is not unfair. I've tried to convince him he needs one for safety, for when he's walking Coleridge, but he always says he's walking with a giant dog and he couldn't be safer if he was walking with a member of MI5."

Harriet wouldn't have gone as far as saying the dog was as good at protection as the British Security Service, but it was true that the sheer size of the bloodhound would deter most anyone with bad intentions.

"And now that I know Coleridge was found wandering the streets..."

"That's unusual too?" Harriet guessed.

"Very," Mrs. Lewis said. "Lord Beresford loves that dog. He would never let him roam free like that. And then there's the study."

"The study?"

Mrs. Lewis nodded. "I'll show you."

Harriet was bewildered, but she followed the housekeeper, drawn both by a sense of obligation and, she had to admit, curiosity. She wanted to see more of this incredible house and to learn more about its reclusive owner.

Mrs. Lewis led her to the left, into a formal drawing room of some kind. The coffered ceilings soared above the marble floors, which were partially covered by several thick area rugs. The walls were covered with the same decorative panels, and two distinct seating areas lay on either side of a massive fireplace with an intricately carved marble mantel. Long velvet curtains framed the windows, and more artwork dotted the walls—moody landscapes, serene still lifes, triumphant battle scenes, representations of Greek and Roman mythology mixed with Impressionist pastoral scenes, and more modern abstract paintings. Harriet wanted to stop and study them, but Mrs. Lewis walked across the parlor and through a doorway on the far side of the room.

Harriet followed her through the doorway and into a room that was smaller, but no less grand. A vast wooden desk was framed by picture windows that looked out over the formal gardens behind the house. A leather-bound book and a sleek silver laptop perched on the top, and a leather-covered desk chair rested behind it, a wool cardigan draped over the back. Two leather club chairs sat across from the desk, with a matching couch nearby. More artwork hung on the walls, and Harriet immediately spotted a small painting of a dog. Coleridge, she was pretty sure, and she recognized it right away as one of her grandfather's pieces.

These observations took a back seat in her mind when she saw that the rug had been pushed up, caught by one of the club chairs as it had been shoved aside. A round wooden table between the club chairs was tipped on its side.

"See the glass there?" Mrs. Lewis asked. Harriet stepped farther into the room and saw what she was pointing at. On the far side of the desk, a smashed glass decanter lay in a dark spot on the rug. "There's something that looks like blood on it."

Harriet bent down and saw that she was right—there was a smear of something dark red on several shards of broken glass.

"That is very strange," Harriet said, straightening up. She suddenly got the sense that she shouldn't touch or disturb anything in the room.

"Do you think something has happened to him?" Mrs. Lewis said. She seemed flustered, overwhelmed, and at a loss as to what to do. Harriet supposed it was no doubt a shock to find the room like this.

"I wouldn't know," Harriet said, just as Coleridge wandered into the room. He sniffed around and then settled himself on the rug in front of the fireplace, resting his head on his front paws. "But this does seem like a bad sign. I can't really imagine how anything good could have led to this." She looked again at the overturned table, the disturbed rug, and the broken glass smeared with something that resembled blood. "If he doesn't typically leave the house—"

"Not like this, he doesn't."

"And with Coleridge left to wander the streets…" As she said it out loud, she realized how bad it all sounded. "If his behavior seems unusual to you, I think it might be worth reporting it to the police."

Mrs. Lewis nodded. "That's what I thought too. I'll give them a call now. I'll let them know that Lord Beresford is missing."

CHAPTER TWO

While Mrs. Lewis placed the call, Harriet stepped forward to study the painting done by her grandfather. She recognized his distinctive realistic style, the soft-edged lines and warm light that always infused his paintings. Many of his paintings had featured animals, so she was sure it was his even before she spotted his signature in the corner of the canvas.

The painting showed a much younger and smaller Coleridge, splayed across a rug in front of the fireplace in this very room. Behind him, a fire burned in the hearth and cast a warm glow over the scene. The dog wore a leather collar studded with bits of metal, which gaped around his puppy-size neck. It was a good likeness of the dog, and a charming image overall.

"I don't know how long he's been gone," Mrs. Lewis was saying into the phone. "The last time I saw him was Friday around noon."

Harriet listened as Mrs. Lewis explained the situation to the person on the other end of the line. "The new lady vet brought his dog back. She said he'd been found on the streets. Lord Beresford would never let Coleridge wander free like that."

Mrs. Lewis was quiet for a moment, and then her tone sharpened. "I've been working at this house since you were in diapers,

Van Worthington. I know when something's wrong. You come out here and see for yourself." She hung up and informed Harriet, "Detective Constable Worthington is on his way. Have you met him?"

Harriet nodded. "I have." She'd gotten to know Van when she got caught up in helping to solve the mystery of the Ravenglen Manor jewel heist.

"His mother is an old friend. Anyway, I don't suppose you need to stick around until he shows up. But I don't know what to do about him." She gestured toward Coleridge.

Harriet turned to the dog. His eyes were big, his posture and face forlorn. "I can take him for now, until Lord Beresford comes back. We have boarding facilities at the clinic."

"Would you?" Mrs. Lewis asked. "I'm sure you'd take better care of him than I could. My husband doesn't like dogs."

Harriet would never understand how someone could dislike dogs, but she kept that to herself. "Of course. Could I grab his things? Like his leash, bed, and food? Familiar things often help a dog feel settled in a new place."

"Come with me." Mrs. Lewis took one last glance around the study then led Harriet through another doorway and into a large room lined with bookshelves and scattered with overstuffed chairs, Coleridge on their heels.

They stepped into a hall and toward a small room that led to what appeared to be a back door. This entryway was far less grand than the front, with chipped tile floors, scuffed white beadboard walls, and hooks holding various coats and hats. Coleridge sat down in the doorway.

"Here's a leash," Mrs. Lewis said, pulling one from a bin. "It's not the one Lord Beresford usually uses though." She dug through the bin but apparently didn't find the leash she was hunting for.

"Is there a collar in there?" Harriet asked.

"Again, not the one he usually uses, but there's this old one." She pulled out a leather collar, and Harriet recognized it right away as the one she'd seen in the picture of puppy Coleridge. "It might be too small."

Harriet took it and moved to Coleridge, who sat still while she fastened the collar around his neck. It still fit, and it didn't seem to make him uncomfortable. She got it fastened and then stroked his head. He was a sweet dog.

"His food is through here," Mrs. Lewis said, leading Harriet and Coleridge out of the mudroom.

They made their way through a narrow room lined with old sinks—a scullery, perhaps—and into a large kitchen that bore some evidence of having been updated decades ago. Oak cabinets were stained dark to enhance the grain, and the floor and counter were both made up of tan square tiles. A busy floral wallpaper and valances over the windows made Harriet feel as if she'd stepped back in time, but in a different way from the rest of the house.

Mrs. Lewis opened a cabinet and loaded cans of food from it into a tote bag. It was a brand Harriet knew and recommended to her patients.

"Does he sleep in a crate?" Harriet asked. "Or a dog bed?"

"No," Mrs. Lewis said. "Lord Beresford usually lets him share his bed. He spoils that dog, I tell you."

No matter how sweet he was, Harriet was not about to let the dog sleep on her bed, but she wouldn't try to get him to sleep in a crate either. He would probably be fine with a dog bed.

"I think that's about it," Mrs. Lewis said, handing the bag to Harriet. "Thank you for taking care of him. I know Lord Beresford will be grateful."

"Hopefully it will only be for a little while," Harriet said. "I'm sure he'll turn up soon."

"Let's hope so."

Harriet and Mrs. Lewis exchanged numbers so the housekeeper could let her know when the dog's master returned, and then Harriet followed the older woman back through the grand rooms to the front of the house again.

She took her leave and walked to the Land Rover, her feet crunching over the crushed shell drive, and opened the door. She got Coleridge settled inside then climbed into the driver's seat and started the engine as a police car pulled into the parking area. Harriet held up a hand in greeting as she passed Van Worthington, and then she cast one last glance at the manor before starting down the long driveway. She kept expecting Mr. Darcy or Lord Grantham to step out, but apparently it was a real lord who lived in that great big house.

Back at Cobble Hill Farm, she took Coleridge into the house, where she unfastened the leash and let him wander around sniffing as he inspected each room.

"You're going to be staying with me for a little while," she explained as she led him into the kitchen and set his food on the counter. Some people thought it was silly to talk to animals, but

Harriet knew they could understand the tone and emotion of a person's voice, if not the words themselves. She did her best to sound calm and confident. "I'm sure you're confused about where your owner is, but he'll be back soon. And I'll take good care of you in the meantime."

She got a bowl, filled it with canned food, and set it on the floor beside a bowl of water. Coleridge quickly wolfed down the entire bowl and then got a drink. Maxwell hurried over, his little wheels squeaking, and Harriet laughed and refilled the bowl.

"You were hungry, weren't you?" She patted Coleridge on the head.

Harriet glanced at the clock on the wall. It was nearly six. She was supposed to have dinner with Aunt Jinny tonight and was due to be over at her place shortly, but she wanted to take Coleridge out for a few minutes before she left. She leashed him again and led him out the back door toward the fenced area behind the barn.

"Go on. Check it out." She unclipped him.

Coleridge sniffed his way tentatively around the yard, and after a few minutes of exploring, she called him back in.

"I'm going to go have my dinner now," she said to the dog as she led him inside. "Make yourself at home. Maxwell and Charlie will show you around, and I'll return in a little while for a walk."

As if he understood, Coleridge moseyed through the house and settled down in front of the fireplace in the living room. Maxwell rushed over to sit near him. Harriet went to the kitchen to wash her hands. She tossed a salad to take to Aunt Jinny's, and then she put on a sweater—even though it was July, Yorkshire would never get as hot as the summers she was used to—and walked across the yard to the dower cottage.

"Hello," Aunt Jinny said when she opened the door. "You know, you don't need to knock or anything. You're family. You can simply come in, especially when I'm already expecting you." She took the salad bowl from Harriet and pulled her into a hug.

"I'll work on it," Harriet said. She was struck once again by how much her aunt reminded her of Dad. They had the same nose, the same chin, the same light-colored hair. It was like looking at a female version of her father. "How are you?"

"I'm good. Busy day seeing patients. With the nicer weather, everyone seems to be getting outside and hurting themselves. I had two sprained ankles and a burn from a grilling incident today."

"I'm sorry to hear that, though I'm glad you're getting business."

"True. And I'm always happy to help." She smiled and led Harriet into her kitchen, a cozy room with ceiling beams, white cabinets, and a terra-cotta tile floor. A large range and worn dining table took up most of the space in the room, and it had the air of a place that had seen many cups of tea and family meals. A pan of something that smelled delicious sizzled on the stovetop. "Anyway, how was your day?"

"Fine until the end, and then it got kind of strange," Harriet said. "Do you know who Liam Beresford is?"

"The baron, right?" Aunt Jinny set the salad on the table and moved toward the range. "He's a part of the landed gentry, if you care about that kind of thing." Her tone of voice made it clear she didn't. "I knew his younger brother, Peter, years ago. Why?"

"Someone brought his dog into the clinic today. It was running around loose." Harriet told Aunt Jinny about what had happened and about her visit to the manor house.

"So the baron is missing?" Aunt Jinny took the pan off the stove and brought it to the table.

"I don't really know," Harriet said. "Mrs. Lewis thinks it's suspicious and called the police. Van showed up to investigate as I was leaving. Mrs. Lewis couldn't take the dog, so I brought him home."

"Liam does love that dog," Aunt Jinny said. "And I suppose that makes sense. He's pretty much Liam's sole companion these days."

"What's his story?" Harriet asked.

"Lord Beresford's?" Aunt Jinny set a pitcher of water and the bowl of salad on the table.

"Yes. I don't really understand what a baron is."

Aunt Jinny chuckled. "Why don't we sit down and pray, and then I'll explain?"

They took their places at the table, and Aunt Jinny asked the Lord to bless the food and their time together. After the prayer, she raised her head. "So, you know about titles, right? The peerage system?"

"I know that in Regency novels everyone wants to marry a duke. I assume that means that's the highest?" Harriet guessed.

"Short of the royal family, which is a whole other ball of wax, I suppose it is. It goes, from highest to lowest, duke, marquess, earl, viscount, baron, baronet."

"So baron's not that high."

"To be included in the peerage at all is meant to be a big deal. Whether it actually is or not is up for debate," Aunt Jinny said.

"And those titles are inherited, right? That's why everyone in the movies is so anxious to have an heir to take over the title and land and such."

"Correct. Some of the titles have been passed down for hundreds of years, while others have been created or died out in that time," Aunt Jinny said.

"It all seems a bit undemocratic. To be handed a ticket to wealth and privilege—or not, based entirely on the circumstances of your birth, which no one can control."

"It isn't all that different from how it works across the pond, is it?" Aunt Jinny countered. "The difference is that instead of titles, it's generational wealth. You all get rich through business or a profession and pass wealth along that way. Some are born into luxury while others aren't."

Harriet couldn't argue with that.

"Besides, not all of them inherit wealth along with the title," Aunt Jinny continued. "Many inherit a pile of crushing debt, as well as the weight of the responsibility of keeping a crumbling estate running."

Harriet picked up her fork and lit into the dish she'd learned was called "bubble and squeak." It was made of whatever was left over from Sunday's meal, which today was cabbage, potatoes, carrots, and roast.

"The Baron Beresford is a title that's been around for hundreds of years," Aunt Jinny said. "The original baron was loyal to the crown and was granted the title and the land after Charles II returned to the throne when Cromwell was defeated in the seventeenth century. The first baron built a house on that land, though it's been rebuilt more than once since that time. The house, land, title, and living—money—has been passed down through the generations. The current Baron Beresford inherited it about thirty years ago, after the death of his father."

"Mrs. Lewis told me he's kind of a recluse."

"That's true. He does mostly keep to himself. I think Dad was one of the few people who really spent time with him."

"Grandad was friends with him?"

"Yes, they were friends for many years. From what I understand, the baron was very interested in art and architecture and things of that sort, so he and Dad had that in common. But Dad was so much older, and Liam was never particularly extroverted. Peter, the younger brother, was always much more friendly and outgoing, but even as a boy, Liam seemed standoffish almost to the point of being rude. But I guess he and Dad saw something in each other."

"Grandad always did like to take in strays," Harriet said.

"Isn't that the truth?" Aunt Jinny chuckled.

"Mrs. Lewis mentioned that his wife passed away," Harriet said. "Does he have children?"

"Two sons, I believe. An heir and a spare, as they say."

Harriet speared a potato. "So the eldest will inherit the title and house someday?"

"I suppose he will. Though I believe he lives in London and isn't around much. I haven't heard or seen anything of him in quite a while."

"Would you have interacted with him much anyway?" Aunt Jinny had attended events at Ravenglen Manor, but Harriet couldn't imagine her down-to-earth aunt enjoying cocktail parties and polo matches with members of the aristocracy.

"Probably not, but typically the heir stays close and is active in the community. Gets involved, shows he cares about the locals, that kind of thing. Raises funds for charity, ingratiates himself."

"It sounds like his father doesn't do a lot of that either." Harriet took another bite.

"True enough. And I suppose he'll inherit either way."

"What if the eldest was a daughter? Would she inherit the title?"

"In some cases, women can inherit titles, and in others, they can't. They changed the law a few years ago to make it easier for women to inherit the crown, but that didn't affect every title. It depended on how they were created back in the day. It's all very steeped in history. I believe this one would pass to the nearest male heir if the baron didn't have a son."

"Are we still living in a world where women don't have the same rights as men? It's so archaic and unfair," Harriet said.

"You aren't the first to say so. There are plenty of people who would like to abolish the peerage system altogether."

"I imagine there's a small but strong minority who are fighting that tooth and nail?"

Aunt Jinny nodded. "I'm sure it'll come as no surprise to you that the people who profit from the system don't want to see it abolished."

Harriet wiped her hands on a napkin. "Do you think there's any chance they would ever abolish it?"

"Who can say? I don't really think about it. It doesn't have much of an impact on my life, nor the lives of most people in England."

The conversation moved on to a funny incident that had happened at Aunt Jinny's clinic that day, and while Harriet enjoyed the rest of the meal, part of her kept thinking about the tradition of inherited titles.

After she'd helped Aunt Jinny clean up from dinner, Harriet said, "I need to take Coleridge for a walk before it gets dark. Any chance you want to come with me?"

"Sure. I could use some exercise. Let me grab a sweater."

A few minutes later they walked back to the big house and Harriet clipped the leash onto Coleridge's collar. Together they started off toward the footpath that led to the cliffs over White Church Bay. As they passed the clinic's parking area, Coleridge started barking. The deep, sonorous sound startled Harriet.

Harriet followed his gaze. "Who's that?" There was a man with brown curly hair by the gallery. He froze when he saw her.

"Who?"

"Over there." Harriet pointed as the man hopped into a little silver car. Coleridge barked again and strained against the leash. "Hello?" Harriet called. "Can I help you?"

The car zoomed backward. She rushed toward it, hoping to—to what? Hoping to stop the man? In his car? She didn't know. But she was certain something wasn't right.

Regardless of how fast she moved, the car was faster. By the time she and Coleridge got to the gallery, all she saw was a cloud of dust as the car disappeared down the driveway.

CHAPTER THREE

For a crazed moment, Harriet thought about chasing after the guy. But she quickly dismissed the idea.

"That was very strange," she said as Aunt Jinny caught up with her.

"Maybe he was delivering a package?" Aunt Jinny suggested. But there were no packages in sight.

"Why would he run, if that was the case?"

"He could be shy. Or afraid of dogs who bark at him."

"Coleridge recognized him," Harriet said. "Whoever it was, Coleridge knew him. It wasn't Liam, was it?"

"No, it wasn't," Aunt Jinny said. "Liam is quite a bit older than that man."

Harriet watched as the cloud of dust dissipated. "Who was that, Coleridge?" The dog gazed up at her. Not for the first time, she wished dogs could talk.

"I'm sure if it's important, we'll find out who it was," Aunt Jinny said.

Harriet hoped she was right, but she had a bad feeling about the whole situation. No one with good intentions ran away like that after being caught lurking around someone's property. Just last month there'd been a prowler spying on her through the gallery window, and she still hadn't quite gotten over the feeling of being watched.

"We're not going to find out what he wanted right now," Aunt Jinny said. "Let's go on our walk and try to forget about this, okay?"

Harriet was still unsettled, but her aunt was right, so she followed her to the footpath once again. Coleridge stood still, gazing at the spot in the distance where the man had disappeared, until Harriet tugged on the leash. Then he relented and came with her.

They walked across the grassy hill that sloped down to the path. Some children played basketball in the driveway of the Danbys' farm. It was a beautiful evening, warm but not too hot, and the sky was filled with a brilliant array of blues, oranges, and pinks as the sun slid lower in the sky.

Once they reached the dirt path, Harriet gazed out over the water sparkling in the setting sun. Boats dotted the surface. Limestone cliffs, dyed golden brown by the evening light, surrounded the bay, and on the narrow strip of beach below, people wandered up and down the shore. During the spring, when the tide was especially low, fossil hunters could be seen along the sea floor, but right now the tide appeared to be on its way in, creeping toward the cliffs a bit more with each cresting wave.

Coleridge sniffed his way along the path, stopping every few feet to examine some enticing smell. The wind whipped along the coastline, and Harriet was glad she'd worn her sweater.

"Summer is my absolute favorite time of year," Aunt Jinny said after taking in a deep breath of the salty sea air. "I love how late it stays light."

"I love summer too," Harriet said. "Especially here, where it's not as hot and sticky as it is back home. Though the beaches in Connecticut have a certain appeal on steamy summer days that you don't find here."

"No, there isn't ever really a time when you want to dunk yourself in the bay," Aunt Jinny agreed. "I'll never forget that summer I came to visit you. Those beaches were the most beautiful I've ever seen, and even though the water was cold, it felt so good."

"But this is beautiful too," Harriet said, gesturing to the beach below. "Not for swimming, but in terms of scenery, it's pretty spectacular."

"It is lovely," Aunt Jinny agreed. "I won't deny that as much as I loved visiting you in the States, my heart is at home in Yorkshire." She chuckled. "Your grandfather hated summer."

"Really?"

"Oh yes. He didn't like the heat, even in our moderate climate. He always complained about it and longed for winter."

"I'll never understand people who love winter," Harriet said. "The cold, the ice, the never-ending snow." She shuddered.

"The warm blankets, the fireplaces, the hot drinks," Aunt Jinny countered. "There was nothing your grandfather loved more than sitting inside on a wintry day and watching the world sleep outside his window."

"I guess everybody's different," Harriet said. They walked along, each lost in her own thoughts, while Coleridge sniffed at everything on the path. All dogs had sensitive noses and explored the world by scent, but that trait was even more pronounced in bloodhounds, and walking with one could be an exercise in patience.

"I talked to Claire Marshall after church yesterday," Aunt Jinny said, breaking the companionable silence. "You've met her, right?"

"Yes, I know who she is." Claire was married with two school-age children she was always chasing and rushing to get to activities after church. "She seems nice. Doesn't she work at the church?"

"Yes, in the office. She mentioned she'd like to have you over for dinner sometime. I said that sounded like a wonderful idea. I think you'd like her, and you should make some friends your own age around here."

"I'm friends with Polly."

"And I'm very happy for you. But you need more than one friend."

"*Is* Claire my age?" Harriet had assumed Claire was several years older than she was. Her hair was threaded with gray, and she often seemed anxious and tired. Harriet wasn't sure what they had in common, aside from attending the same church.

"She's closer to your years than I am," Aunt Jinny said. "Not that I don't like hanging out with you, mind you. But I think you'd enjoy being with some new people too. And Claire is warm, kind, and wonderful."

"Okay." Harriet couldn't really think of what else to say. She didn't see herself and Claire becoming friends, but her aunt was right that she hadn't yet gotten to know very many people in White Church Bay. What could it hurt to get better acquainted with Claire? "That could be fun."

"You'll like her, you'll see." Aunt Jinny smiled.

Coleridge pulled at the leash again, sniffing farther from the path and closer to the edge of the cliff. Harriet started to tug him back when she noticed something. The cliffside seemed to have fallen away up ahead. The path was still intact, but the edge of the cliff was closer to it than she remembered.

"Goodness. Do you see that?" she asked her aunt.

"That's why it's important not to go too close to the edge," Aunt Jinny said. "These old cliffs are slowly eroding, and sometimes big pieces will just break away."

Coleridge continued to pull. Harriet kept a tight hold on his leash but inched closer to see what had him so excited.

"Be careful," Aunt Jinny called from behind her.

"I will." As Harriet got closer to the edge, she could see that quite a large section of the cliff face had fallen. She peeked over and spotted a pile of rocks scattered on the beach. There was also something dark, possibly a piece of clothing. She squinted and determined that it was a shirt, or something with a similar shape, featuring a bold pattern of black-and-gray shapes. "Aunt Jinny, you should come see this."

The shirt was caught on a large piece of driftwood that had washed up against the cliffs. The driftwood had been there as long as Harriet had lived in the area. But she'd never seen clothing caught on it. She thought the item was too big to be a shirt.

Aunt Jinny tentatively crept closer to the edge of the cliff. "Could be a jacket. Probably just…" Her voice trailed off. Something had obviously caught her attention.

"What is it?" Harriet prompted.

"That houndstooth jacket. It's very recognizable. One of a kind, in fact."

"Do you know whose it is?"

Aunt Jinny took a deep breath. "It's Liam Beresford's jacket." She bit her lip and met Harriet's gaze, asking the question foremost in Harriet's mind. "What is it doing at the bottom of the cliff?"

"Do you think he fell?" Harriet asked.

"Liam did walk Coleridge in this area," Aunt Jinny said. "Everyone saw him regularly, usually wearing that coat, though I don't know that he usually came this far."

Harriet guessed they were at least a couple of miles from where Liam would have entered the path near his home. But that didn't seem like an especially long walk for a man with an active dog and nothing but time on his hands.

"He could have gotten too close to the edge and the cliff gave way beneath him," Harriet mused, thinking out loud. It was a horrifying thought, and she took a step back. "It would explain why Coleridge is so interested in this spot. Maybe he was with him when it happened."

At her side, the dog stared down over the edge of the cliff. Harriet couldn't tell if his expression was forlorn, or if that was his usual look.

"But would he have been wearing a jacket in July?" she asked.

"We're both wearing sweaters," Aunt Jinny reminded her. "A light jacket wouldn't be out of place on a cool evening around here." She took a deep breath. "I think we'd better inform Van. You said he was the one who came to investigate at Beresford Manor earlier, right?"

"He was." Harriet pulled her phone out of her pocket and made the call.

Van answered right away. "Hi, Harriet. What can I do for you?"

"Hi, Van. My aunt and I are walking the footpath along the cliffs, and we've found a place where part of the cliff fell away.

Down below is a jacket that might belong to Liam Beresford. I know you went out to his house today when Mrs. Lewis called about him being gone, so we thought we should let you know."

"Tell me exactly where you are."

Harriet did, then told him about how Coleridge had led them to the spot. "He's a bloodhound. They pick up scent trails. He would have recognized his master's scent, though obviously I can't know for sure why he was so interested in this place."

"Okay," Van said. "I'll be there shortly."

While they waited, Harriet and Aunt Jinny came up with a lot of questions. If Liam had fallen off the cliff and died, where was his body? How had his jacket come off? How had Coleridge survived?

On the other hand, if he had fallen from the cliff and survived, why hadn't he come home? Why had he left his jacket behind? And how had he and Coleridge been separated?

The sun was slipping below the horizon when Van arrived in his yellow vest and checker-banded hat, his pale skin flushed. Harriet repeated the story of how they'd come upon the broken cliff face and spotted the jacket below. As she was speaking, two other officers came into view on the beach below, checking out the scene around the jacket. The tide was coming in, so they would need to work quickly.

Van finished taking their statements then told them they were free to go.

"What will happen if it is Liam's jacket?" Aunt Jinny asked.

"We'll launch a full investigation," Van answered.

"Will you let people know he's missing?" Aunt Jinny asked.

"A *full* investigation, Dr. Garrett," he said, tipping his hat.

It was clear they wouldn't get anything else out of him, at least for now. Harriet tugged on Coleridge's leash, and she and Aunt Jinny started home.

"I hope he's all right," Harriet said as they reached the lawn at Cobble Hill Farm.

"Me too." Aunt Jinny's voice was quiet. "I'm sure he'll turn up." But she didn't sound all that sure. As they neared the house, she said, "You're not going to put Coleridge in a kennel, are you?"

After the events of the day—from the strange disappearance and signs of a scuffle at Beresford Manor, to seeing that strange lurker who'd fled the property, to the discovery at the cliffs, Harriet felt unsettled. The stranger especially worried her. What did he want? What if he came back? She knew she'd sleep better with a hundred-pound dog nearby. Bloodhounds generally had amiable natures, which made them terrible guard dogs, but Coleridge had already barked at the man once, so there was a good chance he'd do so again.

"I'd like to keep him in the house, at least for now. I can't bring myself to let him sleep on my bed the way he does with Liam, but we'll both feel better if he's inside."

"I think that's wise."

They said good night, and Harriet went inside and unhooked Coleridge's leash. The dog explored the house, sniffing around each room while Harriet made herself a cup of peppermint tea. She sat down in the study and tried to relax with a book, but she couldn't make herself focus.

She pulled out her phone. It was about nine. That meant it was four in the afternoon at home. Her friend Sylvia would be at her job as a vet tech in the practice where Harriet had worked, but she might answer if things were slow.

Harriet gave her a call, but it went to voice mail. She left a message then got a text from Sylvia. SORRY, THINGS ARE CRAZY HERE, BUT I'LL CALL WHEN I GET OFF WORK.

That wouldn't be for another hour, and Harriet hoped to be in bed by then. She texted back, IT'S NOT IMPORTANT. I'LL TRY YOU AGAIN LATER IN THE WEEK.

Maybe she would try Ellen. Harriet and Ellen had grown up together, and though Ellen commuted to New York City most days for her job in finance and didn't have a lot of free time, she often left the office early to beat traffic. Harriet tried Ellen's number, but it also went straight to voice mail.

Lauren was probably driving her kids around to soccer and ballet practice right about now. Jenn was on vacation in Florida. Who could Harriet call who would have time to talk?

A wave of loneliness washed over her. It was good that her friends back home were living their lives, and she knew it wasn't personal that they weren't free to talk to her right now. The distance and the time difference made it hard.

Maybe Aunt Jinny was right. It could do her good to make some local friends her own age. She and Polly were getting closer, but there was almost a decade between them. Maybe it would be good to spend some time with Claire. Even if they didn't have a lot in common, at least they lived on the same continent. They could start there and find more connections as they continued.

She let Coleridge and Maxwell out one last time and then made sure all the doors and windows were locked.

"There's your bed, but you can sleep where you like," she told Coleridge, who inclined his head as if he understood what she said. "I'm heading upstairs. You let me know if anyone tries to get in."

He thumped his tail on the floor, and she smiled and headed upstairs.

It took her a while to fall asleep. Every noise and creak made her worry someone was breaking in. She reminded herself that Coleridge would alert her if anyone tried to get inside, but it still took her some time to doze off. She slept fitfully, unable to shut off her mind. She finally fell into a deep sleep early in the morning and dreamed of lost dogs—and lost men.

CHAPTER FOUR

When the alarm went off, Harriet felt groggy and disoriented. She stumbled downstairs and found Maxwell in Coleridge's bed and Coleridge sprawled out on the couch. Charlie waited by her food bowl, the tip of her tail flicking impatiently. Both dogs raised their heads as a floorboard creaked under Harriet's foot.

"I feel like you took the invitation to sleep anywhere slightly more literally than I meant it," she informed Coleridge, hands on her hips. The dog gazed up at her, thumping his tail.

Grandad wouldn't have minded the dog being on his furniture. He had loved animals as much or more than she did, if that was possible.

She gave up trying to scold the bloodhound. "Come on. Let's go out, and then I'll get you some breakfast."

She hooked up Maxwell's prosthesis then took both dogs out to the yard and let them run around for a while. She tossed a tennis ball she'd found in a kitchen drawer, and Coleridge brought it back to her a few times. Then she left them in the enclosed dog yard while she brewed a cup of coffee and got ready for the day. Tea was the traditional caffeinated beverage of choice here, and she enjoyed it. But first thing in the morning, she still loved her strong cup of coffee. She let the dogs in and then fed them and Charlie.

While the animals ate, she sat down with her coffee and her Bible to read the passage for the day. She was reading through the story of King Saul's rise and fall and his eventual replacement by David. She turned to 1 Samuel 16, the passage where the prophet Samuel went to the home of Jesse to anoint one of his sons as Israel's future king.

One by one, Samuel rejected each of Jesse's older sons, finally asking Jesse to bring his youngest son in from the fields, where he was guarding the sheep. When Samuel saw him and realized he was the one God had chosen to lead Israel, everyone was surprised, but Samuel reminded them, "People look at the outward appearance, but the Lord looks at the heart." It was a good reminder that things like appearance and wealth—and titles—didn't truly matter. What mattered was a person's heart.

Harriet finished her first cup of coffee right when her phone rang. She answered it, guessing by the time that it was a farmer needing her help with one of their animals. She was right. Laine Richardson had a cow struggling with a difficult labor. Harriet promised to be right there, and she got dressed quickly and headed out.

When Harriet arrived, she found the farmer in more distress than the cow. Harriet soothed both of them, and two hours later, a perfectly healthy calf arrived.

When she walked back into the clinic, Maxwell ran to the front door to greet her, the wheels on his prosthetic squeaking. Charlie perched on the counter and acted like she hadn't noticed her come in. Harriet had left Coleridge in the house, concerned that the new sounds and smells at the clinic might overwhelm him.

"Well, hello there." She bent down to pat the little long-haired dachshund's head.

"You look like you've already had some fun this morning," Polly said from the front desk.

Harriet realized her boots were caked with mud. "Guilty. One second." She stepped back outside to scrape the mud off. When she returned, she explained. "Laine Richardson's cow had a calf."

"Well, that's nice. Hopefully the rest of your day will be a little less exciting. We have a full docket, but nothing out of the ordinary." Polly scrolled through the calendar then tapped the monitor. "Then at four you have an appointment with that reporter from the *Whitby Gazette*."

"Oh, right." In the excitement of the day before, she'd completely forgotten the appointment.

A week earlier a reporter had contacted her about doing a story on the new vet who'd come to take over her grandfather's practice. It was a feel-good piece for the local section of the weekly newspaper, which was largely ads for tourists with a little bit of news sprinkled in.

Harriet hoped the story would bring some good attention to the practice. She knew people were skeptical about a young American woman taking over for the beloved local vet. Some good press might help establish her reputation in the community.

"I'm meeting her at the Crow's Nest, right?"

"That's right," Polly said. "Gemma Loughty. I don't know her. She must be new to the area, so at least you'll have that in common. Anyway, I think your first appointment just arrived."

Elaine Dawson, Doreen Danby's sister, walked toward the clinic door with a cat carrier in her arms.

"It seems Widget has scratched himself in the same spot too much and opened the skin there," Polly said, reading from the screen. "And now he keeps fussing with it and won't let it heal."

"I see." Harriet had seen such cases before. She would check for underlying causes, but she had a good idea of what was going on. "I'll go get the room ready."

She went into the back to prep for the busy day ahead. The appointment with Elaine and Widget went smoothly. There were no underlying skin issues. The wound simply itched while it healed, which made him scratch it more. Harriet gave Elaine a spray that would prevent itching and help the skin heal faster. "If he's still scratching, buy him a onesie," she advised.

Elaine laughed. "Wait, are you serious?"

"As silly as it sounds, a onesie will prevent him from having access to the area, and it'll impede him less than a cone would. There are specially made onesies for cats online. He probably won't like it, but it's a good solution for him. If it hasn't cleared up in a couple of weeks, bring him back, and we'll figure out something else. But I very much doubt you'll have that problem."

Elaine ushered a decidedly grumpy Widget into his carrier. "Thanks, Doc."

The morning was busy with appointments for various dogs, cats, and a pet rat. Then, as Harriet was about to go back to the house to walk Coleridge on her lunch break, Polly waved her toward the front. Van leaned against the counter, chatting with Polly. A woman with sharp green eyes stood next to him, her sleek russet hair brushed back in a ponytail that emphasized her cheekbones.

"Harriet, Detective Constable Worthington and Detective Inspector McCormick have asked to speak with you," Polly said.

Harriet was startled to find officers in her waiting room, but she quickly realized they must be there to talk about the missing baron and his dog. She'd met Kerry McCormick before. She was from the regional office and only got involved in major crimes. Harriet supposed the missing baron qualified.

She smiled at Van and DI McCormick. "Hello. Why don't you come on back to my study?"

"Thank you," DI McCormick said.

Harriet led them into the house and to her study. She was still cleaning and organizing the small room, which her grandfather had left stuffed to the gills with papers and files. Polly kept the front desk and the main filing cabinets meticulous, but Harriet had asked her to leave her grandfather's records alone so she could go through them herself.

Harriet sat down at the desk chair and indicated the two chairs across from the desk, where the officers made themselves comfortable.

"We'd like to ask you a few questions about Liam Beresford, if you don't mind." DI McCormick's tone made it clear that Harriet didn't really have a choice.

"That's fine," Harriet said. "I'm afraid I won't be much help though. I've never met the man."

"I understand that, but you're still involved, if not directly. How did you end up at Beresford Manor yesterday, when DC Worthington was called to investigate the disappearance?"

"A gardener named Archie Osbourne brought a dog into the practice yesterday afternoon," Harriet explained. "Mr. Osbourne found him in town and brought him to me, hoping he was chipped, which would tell us who he belonged to."

The inspector nodded as she took notes.

"We weren't able to locate a chip, but Polly recognized him as Coleridge, Lord Beresford's bloodhound," Harriet went on. "I tried calling the baron, but there was no answer, so I went to Beresford Manor to return the dog to him. When I got there, I met his house-keeper, Mrs. Lewis, who seemed to think something had happened to Lord Beresford. She said it was very odd that he was gone and that there were signs he'd been gone for a few days. She was worried enough to think it was worth calling the police."

"How did you know to search for clues regarding Lord Beresford's disappearance in his study?" DI McCormick asked.

"I didn't," Harriet said. "I'd never been to the house before. Mrs. Lewis showed me the room and asked if I thought it looked suspicious."

"Why would she think you might know if it looked suspicious?"

"I don't know," Harriet said, trying not to get flustered by the line of inquiry, which seemed to imply that she was sticking her nose where it didn't belong—or that she might even be involved. "I'd never met her before yesterday. But she was very upset. I think she wanted someone to verify what she was seeing, and I was the one who happened to be there."

"And did you think it was suspicious?"

"I told her that I thought it was, because the room was in dis-array," Harriet said. "Again, I've never met Lord Beresford—hadn't even heard of him before yesterday—so I didn't really know."

The inspector looked up from her notes. "Did you touch anything in the study?" she asked.

"No," Harriet said.

"You didn't try to get into his laptop?"

"No. Why would I?"

"Do you know what the password is?"

"I haven't the slightest idea."

"We have our techs trying to get into it," Van said. "But if you know the password—"

"I've never met the baron, so how could I know his computer password?" Harriet asked.

"How long did you stay at Beresford Manor yesterday?" DI McCormick asked, ignoring Harriet's question.

"I don't know. Maybe fifteen minutes?" Harriet said. "Long enough to talk to Mrs. Lewis and gather some supplies for Coleridge. She wasn't sure what to do with the dog, so I said he could stay with me until his owner came back."

"And why was that?"

"Why did I say he could stay with me?" Harriet stared at the inspector. Was a good deed suspicious somehow? "Because I'm a vet, and I have kennels on my property. I know how to take care of all kinds of animals. I frequently board dogs when their owners go out of town. It seemed to make sense."

"You didn't have any other reason to keep the dog close?" DI McCormick asked.

"I truly don't understand what other reason I could have," Harriet said. "I mean, he's a very nice dog and all, but I have two pets of my own already. I took him because he needed somewhere to stay, the only other person there at the time couldn't take him, and I happen to have the facilities to care for him until his owner is located."

DI McCormick narrowed her eyes. "Can you tell me how you came across Lord Beresford's jacket on the beach last night?" she asked.

"That was Coleridge's doing," Harriet answered. "My aunt and I took him for a walk last night. He led us to the edge of the cliff, where we could see that some of the cliff face had fallen in. The jacket was below it."

"How did you recognize the jacket as belonging to Lord Beresford, if you'd never met him?" DI McCormick seemed to think she'd caught Harriet in a trap somehow.

"I didn't," Harriet replied evenly. "My aunt did."

If the inspector felt any kind of disappointment, she hid it well. "How could your aunt see the coat well enough to recognize it from that high up?"

"It was easy enough to see the color and the pattern. It was black and gray checks."

"It's houndstooth," Van said.

"Houndstooth then," Harriet repeated, though she wasn't sure why the exact name of the pattern mattered. "I never saw it up close, and I can't verify that it was his coat," she added. "But since my aunt was sure it belonged to Lord Beresford and we knew he'd been reported missing, we thought we should call it in, in case it could somehow provide you a lead to find him."

"How do you think the jacket ended up on the beach?" the inspector asked.

"My aunt said Lord Beresford often walked his dog along the cliff trail. And given how Coleridge was drawn to that spot where the cliff had given way, we worried that he'd fallen there."

"What made you think the dog was drawn to that spot?" Van asked.

"He led us toward it," Harriet repeated. She understood that the police often asked the same question in different ways to make sure a person wasn't lying, but it was starting to annoy her. "Coleridge is a bloodhound. All dogs pick up scents, but bloodhounds are especially good at it, having been bred for it. If Lord Beresford was at the cliff edge, it would make sense for Coleridge to be drawn to that spot."

"I see." DI McCormick scribbled in her notebook again. "And what did you do after you reported the jacket?"

"We waited for Van there. After we talked to him, we went home."

"Have you heard from Lord Beresford?" Van asked.

"No. I left my number with his housekeeper so he can contact me about his dog whether the clinic is open or not. I've heard he's very fond of his dog, and I would understand his anxiety to get Coleridge back as soon as possible."

The inspector met Harriet's gaze. "You must see how strange it appears—that within a couple months of you moving to town, the baron goes missing, and you're the one who finds not only his dog, but also his jacket."

"I suppose I was in the right occupation at the right time for someone to bring me a lost dog," Harriet said. "Or the wrong one at the wrong time, which is how it's starting to feel."

DI McCormick's gaze didn't falter.

Harriet was beyond ready for the interview to be over. "If there's anything I can do to help find the baron, please let me know. Coleridge misses him, and I'd like to reunite them as soon as possible."

"Have you ever heard of the group End Peerage Now?" Van asked.

"No, but based on the name, I assume they're against inherited titles."

"That's correct," Van said.

"Until yesterday I didn't even know where baron fell in the ranking of aristocratic titles," Harriet said. "We don't have them in the States, of course, and I haven't interacted with anyone titled since moving here. It hasn't come up between the move, taking over my grandfather's practice, and going through his house."

Neither officer said anything for a moment. Finally, DI McCormick cleared her throat. "Is there anything else you can think of that might be important for us to know?"

Harriet thought for a moment. "Actually, yes," she said. "Last night, when Aunt Jinny and I started out on the walk with Coleridge, there was a man on our property. He was in the driveway in front of the art gallery. Coleridge recognized him, but when I called out to see what the man wanted, he got into a silver car and drove off."

"Can you describe the man?"

"He had curly brown hair. That was really all I could see."

"Any idea who he was?"

"None," Harriet said. "And I have no idea what he was doing there, how Coleridge knew him, or why he ran away when I called out to him."

"Why didn't you mention this last evening?" Van said. "When I talked to you about the jacket?"

"I was too upset by the idea that the baron had fallen off the cliff. Plus I had no idea why the man was at the house. He might have simply been lost, and Coleridge's bark scared him off."

"Did anyone else see this man?" the inspector asked.

"My aunt Jinny was with me," Harriet said. "She saw him too. You can ask her."

"We're planning to speak with Dr. Garrett," Van said.

"Anything else, Dr. Bailey?" DI McCormick asked.

"Not that I can think of."

DI McCormick put the cap back on her pen. "If you think of anything else, please let us know."

"I will." Harriet stood and walked the two officers out through the clinic. When the door closed behind them, she sighed and massaged her temples, where a headache was beginning to form.

Polly was—under Charlie's close supervision—unpacking a new shipment of the canned cat food they kept on hand. "They can't possibly think you had something to do with this, but your reaction makes me think they've given you that impression," she said to Harriet.

"I don't know," Harriet said. "I suppose they have to explore every possibility."

"But why would you have anything to do with Lord Beresford? You didn't even know who he was."

Harriet shrugged. "It's okay. I truly don't know anything, so no matter how hard they probe, they're not going to find any secrets I'm hiding."

"But they should be searching for him and trying to figure out what actually happened, not harassing someone who was dragged into it and has been trying to help."

Harriet couldn't argue with her. "Thanks, Polly. I'm going to take Coleridge for a walk and then get some lunch."

"Okay. I'll wait until you get back to take my lunch," Polly said. "I have some invoices to handle after I finish with these boxes."

Harriet gestured to the box where Charlie had made herself a bed. "You'd better not mess with that one. It's been claimed."

"I'll let her stay there for now," Polly said, smiling at the calico cat. "She looks too happy to kick her off it."

Charlie closed her eyes and purred as if in confirmation.

Harriet found Coleridge curled up in an armchair in the living room. He lifted his head when she walked in, and she saw a flash of hope in his eyes, but then he lowered his head onto his paws.

"I'm sorry, buddy. It's just me." She knelt in front of the dog and held out her hand to let him sniff it. "We're trying to find your friend though. Hopefully, you'll be reunited with him soon enough." She stroked his head and then stood up again. "Come on. Let's go for a walk."

Coleridge must have recognized that word, because he hopped up and followed Harriet into the kitchen, where she'd left his collar and leash. The collar wasn't all that tight on him, but she thought he'd be more comfortable without it unless they were on a walk.

She picked up the collar to put it on him—and that was when she noticed something. There were words engraved inside. She held it up to the window and read, *Love from Daisy*.

Who was Daisy? The baron's late wife? She thought back, trying to remember if she'd heard the name of the baroness.

Harriet realized she was letting herself get distracted, so she focused on fastening the collar around Coleridge's neck. He thumped his tail on the ground, eager to get outside. She clipped on the leash, and they got moving.

But as she stepped out the front door, something caught her eye. Movement at the edge of the yard.

Harriet had barely registered the curly hair and the black jacket before Coleridge barked and took off, yanking the leash right out of her hand.

CHAPTER FIVE

Harriet hoped the dog would catch the man who'd been lurking around the house, but he was gone by the time Coleridge made it to the stone fence that edged the property. The low whine of an engine told her how he'd managed to get away again.

Nothing about the situation told her who the man was or what he wanted. Harriet stood still, blood pumping in her ears, her heart racing, while she considered what to do. Finally, she took her phone out of her pocket and dialed Van Worthington's number.

"Harriet?" He was in a car, judging by the sound of a blinker.

"He was here again. The man with the curly hair. He was hanging around outside the house, and when Coleridge saw him, he took off after the guy," Harriet said. "But he got away in a car again."

"Why would he hang around your property, only to run when he sees you and the dog?" Van mused, as if to himself.

"I don't know," Harriet said. "But I sure would love to find out. If he knows Coleridge, it makes sense he must have something to do with Liam Beresford's disappearance."

"Hang on." Van's voice became muffled, as if he'd covered the mouthpiece. He was probably speaking to DI McCormick. Then his voice came through clearly once more. "We're on our way back to you. Don't go anywhere, all right?"

"Okay." Coleridge would be disappointed not to go for his walk, but he would have to wait. "I'll be here."

Harriet let Coleridge nose around outside until she figured the officers were almost to the farm, then she called the dog into the house. Her lunch break was nearly over, and she hoped Van and DI McCormick would hurry up, or she would have to keep some of her afternoon patients waiting. She made herself a sandwich, and while she ate, she opened her laptop and typed the words *End Peerage Now* into her web browser.

The first result led her to a website for a group that, as their name stated, wanted to end the peerage system that conferred inherited titles. The site, which had an amateurish quality to it, with simple lists of links and basic colors, seemed to belong to a group that stridently opposed the system, which it labeled as "unfair, unjust, and unconscionable."

She poked around on the site for information about how exactly the group protested the existence of the aristocracy, but she couldn't find anything about their activities, nor its members or leadership.

Whoever they were and whatever they did, they weren't especially open about it. She did, however, find a page that listed current aristocratic titleholders. There were more than she had thought. It was hard to imagine that there were hundreds of dukes, marquesses, earls, and barons walking around England, but apparently there were over four hundred barons alone. And the site listed the addresses of their ancestral homes.

She skimmed the list and found Baron Beresford, with the address of Beresford Manor in Yorkshire. Anyone who wanted to know where he lived could find it.

She clicked on a link that took her to a message board. She scanned the entries, finding some discussion about organizing various protests, but the site didn't seem to be especially active, so she went back to the main search page.

Below the first link was another that brought Harriet to a website for a London newspaper. Protests Disturb House of Lords Meeting, the headline read. A quick search in a second browser window confirmed that the House of Lords was the branch of Parliament historically made up of landed gentry. It seemed that wasn't entirely the case anymore, and not all of the seats were passed down with an inherited title, but some of them were. Which meant that instead of being elected to their seats in government, those people inherited them along with their houses and land and titles.

She clicked back to the other tab and read the article, which reported that a recent meeting of the House of Lords had been interrupted by the group End Peerage Now. Some members had burst into the chamber carrying signs and shouting slogans before they were subdued and arrested.

She clicked on the next link, which led to a couple of articles about End Peerage Now protesting at a courthouse and then during a summer festival at some duke's house.

Harriet was so wrapped up in her research that the knock on her door surprised her. She closed the laptop and got up to answer it. Coleridge raised his head from his spot on the rug.

DC Worthington and DI McCormick didn't seem pleased to be there again.

"Thanks for coming." Harriet stepped out onto the front step and pointed to the gallery. "That's where I saw him, and he drove toward the road."

"Did you see him better this time?" Van asked.

"I could see curly brown hair again," Harriet told him. "He had on a black jacket, but I couldn't see anything else. He moved so quickly."

"Was he coming toward the house?" DI McCormick asked.

"I'm not really sure. I assumed so, but I don't know."

The police officers looked at each other and then back to Harriet.

"You came out of the house, and then what happened?" the inspector asked.

"Coleridge saw him first. Or smelled him, I don't know. But he took off after the guy, who hopped in his car and drove away."

"This was the second time you saw this man, correct?" DI McCormick asked.

"That's right. The first was last night, which went the same way. Coleridge recognized him and started barking, and he fled."

"Do you have any idea who the man might be?"

"I don't. I don't think I've seen him before this."

"Do you have any idea what he wanted?" Van asked.

Harriet had formed an idea. "I think he was here to steal Coleridge."

Both police officers seemed confused by Harriet's idea.

"You think the man came here to kidnap the dog?" Van asked.

"Yes. That's what makes the most sense, really. Why else would he be here again?"

Finally, DI McCormick spoke. "Why don't we step inside, and you can tell us more about your theory?"

The way she said it, it was clear she didn't necessarily buy Harriet's idea, but at least she was willing to listen. Harriet led them inside the house and to the living room. She gestured for them to sit on the couch, and she took one of the club chairs. Coleridge sniffed the air from his spot by the fireplace, but he didn't get up.

"You think the man who ran away as soon as he saw you and the dog was here to kidnap the dog?" DI McCormick asked.

When she said it like that, it did sound kind of strange.

"His appearance must be connected to Coleridge being here," Harriet said. "And Coleridge knows who this man is, based on how he responds."

"Why would anyone want to kidnap a dog?" Van asked.

"Oh, he's quite valuable," Harriet said. "I'm assuming he's a purebred, in which case he's worth hundreds of dollars—or pounds, rather."

"A dog is worth that much?" Van's mouth hung open.

"They can be worth far more, but that's my best guess," Harriet said.

"You're not sure he's a purebred, though, right?" DI McCormick pointed out. "That would make a difference in his valuation, wouldn't it?"

"It would," Harriet said. "He wouldn't be worth nearly as much if he's not."

"Is there any way to find out? If that's a potential motivation here, it would be important to know."

"You're right. I'll look into that. But the reason someone is after him may not be monetary," Harriet said. "Someone could want him because he belongs to the missing baron. I don't know if they want leverage against him or something else along those lines. Maybe Coleridge saw the man kidnap his owner, and now the man wants to get rid of the dog who can identify him, or—"

"How could the dog identity him?" DI McCormick interrupted.

"He's a bloodhound, remember? If that man had something to do with Lord Beresford's disappearance, and Coleridge was nearby at the time, he would recognize the man's scent."

They still didn't seem convinced, but the inspector made notes on her pad again. Harriet suspected the police officer didn't believe any of what she was saying. "If the man you saw came here to kidnap the dog, why hasn't he done so yet?"

"I think he hoped to sneak up and take the dog before anyone noticed him," Harriet said. "But in both cases, he lost the element of surprise."

"Didn't you say you let go of the leash today?" DI McCormick said. "Why wouldn't he take the dog when it ran toward him?"

"I suppose because he knew he'd been seen," Harriet said. "He couldn't risk it. And he couldn't exactly scoop up a hundred-pound barking dog. I think he'll try again some other time."

The inspector didn't say anything, but she took notes. As Harriet answered her questions, she didn't know if the officer believed her theory, but at least she treated Harriet less like a suspect.

"Do you have any kind of security system here?" Van asked.

"I'm afraid not," Harriet said.

"The doors and windows lock, though, right?"

"Yes," Harriet said. "And now that I know what the man wants, I will for sure keep Coleridge in the house with me." She contemplated whether the kennels might be safer, since he would be locked inside, but anyone truly dedicated to dognapping would find a way to get into the cages. She had better keep him as close to her as possible.

"That might be wise," DI McCormick said. Then she asked, "Do you feel safe keeping the dog with you, given all that's happened?"

Harriet realized they were giving her an out. If she said she was afraid, they would try to find another situation for Coleridge.

But she didn't want an out. Now that she thought she knew what the man was after, she was invested. Someone wanted this dog. And that someone no doubt knew something about the missing baron. As long as she had the dog, she might be able to figure out what the connection was. Besides, Coleridge had been through enough, and if she could prevent anything else from happening to him, she would.

"I'll keep him here," she said. "The good thing is that he's very big and very loud. It wouldn't be easy to take him quietly."

At first, she thought they might argue with her. If the man did want to get his hands on Coleridge, the dog would be safer in police custody—and she would be safer too. But she could also see that neither of them was quite sure what to do with such a large dog or how the police would manage him.

"I'm a veterinarian," Harriet reminded them. "He'll be better off in my care than in some cage at the station."

That argument seemed to work, as DI McCormick capped her pen and stood up. "Right. Well, if you see this suspicious fellow again, please call and report it right away."

"I will."

By the time the officers left for the second time, Harriet was officially running late. She put Coleridge on a leash and took him with her into the clinic.

Polly was at her desk. Charlie hopped from the cardboard box onto the desk to meow a greeting at Harriet then glared at her companion. Coleridge watched the cat calmly, allowing an excited Maxwell to sniff him in greeting.

Polly nodded to the dog. "New partner at the practice?"

"I'm going to keep him close for a while. He'll hang out here with us this afternoon."

"That's fine with me, but Charlie may need some convincing." Polly reached out to stroke the cat's fur, soothing her. Charlie started to purr but kept her eyes focused on the big dog. "Were the police here again?"

Harriet realized she hadn't told Polly what was going on. She filled her friend in and warned her to keep an eye out for the man with the curly brown hair. "Does he sound like anyone you recognize?"

Polly shook her head. "I mean, most of the men in this town have brown hair. It could be anyone."

"True enough."

Harriet set Coleridge up in the surgery room. She fashioned a bed for him from extra blankets and made sure he had fresh water, and then she locked the door and deposited the key in her pocket. No one would be able to get him out of there without her knowledge. She would check on him often to make sure he didn't get too lonely.

The afternoon passed quickly, with the normal array of patients, and soon it was time for Polly to head home. The clinic was clean and quiet, and Maxwell and Charlie had been let into Harriet's house for the evening.

"Don't forget your interview at four," Polly said before stepping out the door.

"Oh, right." It was a good thing Polly had reminded her. She might have forgotten in all the excitement.

"I don't think they'll let you take Coleridge into the Crow's Nest," Polly continued. "What are you going to do with him?"

That was a very good question. She was wary about letting Coleridge out of her care, knowing there was a possible dognapper on the loose.

"I guess I'll have to leave him at home," she said uneasily.

"Or you could let me take him home, and then you can pick him up after your interview," Polly suggested. "Good thing Mum was fine with me using the car today."

"Are you sure? I wouldn't want to impose—on you or your parents." Polly still lived at her parents' house.

"They're used to me bringing home every stray I come across," Polly said. "They were the least surprised of anyone when I started working at a vet clinic. They won't mind if I bring him home for a couple of hours. I have to head out around six thirty for a date, but if you pick him up before then, it shouldn't be a problem."

Harriet was dying to ask about Polly's date—her assistant had a very active social life—but she figured if Polly wanted her to know about it she would tell her. So all she said was, "If you're sure."

"Of course."

Harriet unlocked the door to the clinic, waking Coleridge from what must have been a lovely nap, and helped Polly load him into the back seat of the car she shared with her mother. Polly often biked to work, so it almost felt serendipitous that she hadn't today. Harriet waved and watched them drive off then returned to the office. She was pretty sure Coleridge was a purebred bloodhound, but she wanted to try to confirm that. If he was, money might be a motive for someone wanting to kidnap him.

She sat down at the computer in the office. Most of the current patient records were in the database, though many of the older records were in her grandfather's study. She found and read Coleridge's file, thinking that if Grandad had known whether Coleridge was purebred, he would have made a note of it.

Coleridge was nearly four years old and weighed forty-eight kilograms at his last visit, which meant he was just over a hundred pounds. The owner was listed as Liam Beresford, and the address was right. Grandad had made a note that Coleridge had come from Lyons Breeders. It was a pretty safe bet he was a purebred then. It also tracked for her that an English lord would have a purebred dog. Maybe she was relying on stereotypes, but it seemed appropriate somehow. Still, it wasn't proof. If the police needed proof that Coleridge was purebred, she would need to search elsewhere.

She started to click out of the record, but then she saw something else in the file. *Conditions—Food Sensitivities.* From there, it listed specific things that Coleridge had allergic reactions to. It was a common enough condition and easy to treat with medication. But the medication Grandad had prescribed had to be taken every twenty-four hours, and Harriet hadn't given Coleridge any since he'd been in her care.

Mrs. Lewis must have forgotten to give the medicine to her, or maybe she just didn't know about the condition. Harriet got the sense the housekeeper wasn't responsible for feeding or caring for the dog, so she might not have even known to look out for it. They had the medication on hand at the clinic, and the easy thing to do would be to grab some, but the proper thing to do would be to retrieve Coleridge's prescription and use that up before refilling it. Fortunately, it was merely a medication that protected Coleridge from accidental allergen ingestion. His regular food was safe for him to eat without issues.

Still, she'd feel better if he was back on the medicine. She picked up her phone and scrolled until she found Mrs. Lewis's number.

Mrs. Lewis answered promptly. "Hello?"

"Hi, Mrs. Lewis, this is Harriet Bailey, the veterinarian."

"Oh, hello. How is Coleridge? Is there any news about Lord Beresford?"

"I don't know if there's any update on Lord Beresford." Harriet decided not to worry her with the suspicion about the cliff for now, nor the strange man she suspected of trying to steal Coleridge. "But Coleridge is doing fine. He's a sweetie. I just had a question about him. I went through his file, and I saw that he takes a medication for his food allergies. Would you mind if I swing by the manor to pick it up?"

"Goodness me, he does. I'm sorry. I was so distracted yesterday I didn't even think about that. How is he doing? Is he okay?"

"He's fine," Harriet repeated. "He's only missed a day or two at this point." Actually, she didn't know how many days he'd missed, she realized. It depended on when Lord Beresford had disappeared and who had administered his medication. "But if I could come by and get the medication, that would be great."

"Of course. I can't run by the manor house tonight to pick it up, unfortunately. I've got my grandson, but would tomorrow suit?"

It wouldn't hurt Coleridge to go another night without the medication. Harriet was careful about what the animals in her care had access to. "That should be fine. What time is good for you?"

"My computer isn't working at the moment—not since my grandson spilled apple juice on it, bless his heart—and my calendar is on there, so I'm kind of flying blind. I don't know. What works for you?"

Harriet checked her schedule, and they agreed to meet at the Manor House at eleven the next morning. She locked up the clinic and headed home to change out of her work clothes before going to meet the reporter at the pub.

Now all she had to do was manage to not embarrass herself in the press.

CHAPTER SIX

Harriet pulled on slim-fitting jeans and a short-sleeved peacock-blue blouse paired with ballet flats and gold earrings. She brushed her hair and added a touch of lipstick before she headed out. She was nervous about talking to a reporter, but at least she wasn't wearing muddy boots and work pants anymore. It would be fine. She could talk about taking over the vet practice without saying anything too embarrassing. Couldn't she?

She drove out of the driveway and down the steep and narrow streets of White Church Bay. It was such a perfect little English fishing village, the streets lined with small shops and beautiful historic homes built right up against the road. At this time of year, the place was clogged with tourists and day-trippers, but Harriet didn't mind. She understood why they were drawn to the area's serene, natural beauty and the picturesque village.

She found a parking spot in the upper part of town. From here, she could see out over the bay. She stood still, enjoying the view of the water, the people walking on the beach, and the boats coming in and out of the harbor.

There was a cluster of boats closer to shore than she usually saw, and one of them trailed a large net as it slowly moved parallel to the shore. Harriet felt queasy as she realized what they were doing. The boats were near the part of the shoreline where the coat had been found. They were dragging the bay—for a body.

Harriet turned away and started toward the steps that led to the lower part of town. She prayed they wouldn't find one. She had to hold out hope that Lord Beresford was out there somewhere and would soon come home safe and sound.

She tried to focus on the upcoming interview as she made her way down the steep stairs. *Just be yourself*, she told herself. *But maybe more charming.*

It really was a beautiful little village, and she took in the sights as she walked past the charming bookshop with the picture window filled with old and new finds, the florist where the sweet blooms tempted her even from the sidewalk, and the antiques shop brimming with artifacts from the past. Someday she would have time to explore all the shops and places to eat along this stretch.

"Harriet!" Claire Marshall came her way with paper grocery sacks under one arm. Her button-down was mostly tucked into her slacks, and her hair was pulled back into a ponytail, but the wisps that had escaped had been blown about by the wind and frizzed by the humidity.

"Hi, Claire." Harriet was surprised to see her without her children.

"It's good to see you." Claire smiled. "How are things going? Are you settling in all right?"

"I am. Thanks for asking," Harriet said. "How about you?"

"I'm fine," she said, brushing her hair back with her free hand. "I spent most of my paycheck on oat milk and dairy-free biscuits, but you know, aside from that, I'm doing great."

"Dairy-free?"

"My youngest has so many food allergies that I have to shop at the specialty grocer down here. It costs a fortune."

"I'm sorry to hear that," Harriet said, unsure how else to respond.

Claire shrugged. "What are you going to do? You gotta take care of your kids. Anyway, did your aunt mention we would love to have you over sometime?"

"She did," Harriet said. "That's so kind."

"It's purely selfish, I assure you. It's not very often that someone young and fun moves to town."

Harriet laughed. "When were you thinking?"

"How about Friday?" Claire asked. "Maybe you could come around the house and we could throw something on the grill?"

Harriet smiled, though she wasn't so sure. She would want to contribute to the meal, of course, but what could she bring that wouldn't aggravate Claire's child's allergies? And what could they possibly have to talk about that would last more than five minutes?

But she needed to meet people, like Aunt Jinny said. She could have dinner. Perhaps they would stumble upon common ground and be fast friends by the end of the evening.

"That sounds great," Harriet said. "What time? And what should I bring?"

"Would six suit?" Claire asked.

"It would."

"Fabulous. I'll text you the address. And no need to bring anything. We'll have—" Claire was interrupted by her phone, and she pulled it out and read the screen. "My oldest. I'm sorry, but I need to grab this."

"No problem."

"We'll see you at six on Friday," Claire said, just before she put the phone to her ear.

Harriet waved as Claire continued. They had nothing in common, and if dinner at Claire's was as chaotic as that short encounter, Harriet would need to go on a long walk to wind down afterward. But she would never cure her loneliness by staying in all the time, so she would give Friday's dinner her best.

Harriet continued to where the Crow's Nest sat near the end of a stretch of shops and restaurants. She took a deep breath as she pushed open the heavy wooden door and stepped inside. The old pub had rough-hewn wooden floors worn smooth through the years, and its low ceiling and timbered walls indicated the building's age. The walls were hung with mirrors and prints showcasing the town's maritime past, and a large fireplace gave the space a warm, welcoming feel.

Harriet scanned the space for someone who could be Gemma, and spotted a young woman at a corner table. She had brown hair that fell in soft waves around her face and wore a stylish blazer and jeans. She smiled and waved when she saw Harriet.

Harriet crossed the room, already feeling more at ease. Gemma was about her age, maybe a few years younger, and her expression was friendly and open.

"Hello. You must be Harriet. I'm Gemma." She stood as Harriet neared, and held out her hand. "It's nice to meet you."

Harriet was still new at deciphering the differing English accents, but it wasn't hard to place Gemma as being from London or some other posh area of the country. In any case, Gemma wasn't from Yorkshire.

"Harriet Bailey." She shook Gemma's hand and noticed her makeup was understated but perfectly applied. "It's nice to meet you."

"It's great to meet you as well. What can I get you?"

"A Coke, please."

Gemma cocked her head. "You sure? I'm paying."

Harriet laughed. "I'm sure. Thank you though."

"Two Cokes then. I'll be right back." Gemma went to the bar and returned with two glasses of soda. She set one in front of Harriet then slid around the table and sat down across from her. "So. How do you like England?"

"It's been wonderful, so far anyway," Harriet said. "I'm still adjusting to—well, everything. Driving on the wrong side of the road for one."

"I totally get that. I went on a holiday to South Carolina last year with some friends, and we about died. Nearly caused several accidents trying to remember to stay on the right side of the road. I don't know how you all do it over there."

Harriet laughed. "How did you choose South Carolina?" It was a lovely state but not necessarily known as a hot spot for visitors from the UK.

"My friend Darcie dated a man from Charleston for a while and became addicted to some of the food. We went to South Carolina for some good American barbecue."

"Did you find any?"

"I think I ate my weight in pork while we were there. It was amazing. And the American South is beautiful."

"It is," Harriet agreed. "Next time, you should go to the Northeast, where I'm from. Connecticut is beautiful in a different way from the South." In her mind, she pictured the rolling hills, the historic colonial-style homes, and the charming little villages that dated back hundreds of years.

"I'd love to see it sometime. I've been to New York City, but I haven't seen much of the rest of that part of the country. Maybe you can show me sometime."

"Maybe I will." Harriet was enjoying their conversation immensely. She had been nervous for nothing. Gemma was a reporter, but she was also a fellow human being, and a nice one at that.

"What are your impressions of Yorkshire?" Gemma asked.

"It's beautiful," Harriet said. "It's such a lovely part of the world. I'm eager to explore the moors, and I'd love to see more of the villages up and down the coast."

"It is pretty here, isn't it?" Gemma smiled. "I'm rather new to the area as well. I moved to Whitby about six months ago for this job, and it's such a change from London, but there's something calming about it. Like my spirit can breathe here."

"That's a good way to say it," Harriet said. "My soul can breathe here too. Not that I came from a big city. Coventry is pretty rural once you get outside the village, like it is here."

"Tell me about where you came from. How did you grow up in America when your grandfather was British?"

Harriet told Gemma how her father had been raised in Yorkshire but came to the States for college, where he'd met her mother, who was studying to be a nurse. "They fell in love, and they settled in Connecticut, near her family," Harriet said.

"Isn't that always the way?" Gemma said. "My sister fell in love with a man from Sweden of all places, and now they live in Stockholm, and we hardly ever see her."

"I hear Sweden is lovely though." Harriet didn't know much about it, but she envisioned a lot of trees and snow.

"It is. And she's happy. Maybe I'm jealous because I haven't found the man who would make me drop everything and move to another country." Gemma sipped her soda. "How about you? Did you leave behind a boyfriend who's pining for your return?"

"The opposite, in fact." Harriet traced her finger through the condensation on her glass. "Part of the reason I decided to move was a broken engagement. I needed a fresh start, and this seemed like an ideal one."

"A broken engagement sounds very dramatic."

"It wasn't, really. I mean, of course, I was heartbroken. We'd been together for so long—since vet school—and everyone assumed we'd get married and start our own practice. But then he ended it, and we worked to disentangle our lives, and in the middle of that, my grandfather died and left me his vet practice. It seemed like the right move, much as I miss Grandad."

Gemma asked questions about what it was like for Harriet to take over her grandfather's practice, whether it was different to treat animals in the UK, and what she liked and didn't like about living in her grandfather's home. The reporter was smart, witty, and relatable. It turned out Gemma was also an only child and a history buff, and she too missed the group of friends she'd left behind to move to Yorkshire.

"Another round?" Gemma asked, indicating their empty glasses.

"I probably shouldn't," Harriet said. "I have to go pick up a dog and take him home. The receptionist at the clinic took him for a while, but I need to grab him so she can make her dinner plans."

"Your dog?" Gemma cocked an eyebrow.

"No, not my dog. It's a strange story." Harriet stopped herself. Gemma was fun to talk to, but she was a reporter. Harriet wasn't sure the news about Liam Beresford was public. On the other hand, the police hadn't told her *not* to tell anyone.

"Go on." Gemma folded her hands together and rested them under her chin, smiling up at Harriet.

"The dog actually belongs to Liam Beresford. Lord Beresford, the baron. He lives in a big old manor house like something out of a Jane Austen novel."

"Like Northanger Abbey, or more like Pemberley?"

"Goodness. Not as grand as either of those." Harriet thought for a moment. "More like Norland Park in *Sense and Sensibility*."

Gemma raised her eyebrows again. "That's grand enough for me. But why do you have his dog?"

Harriet decided it couldn't hurt to tell Gemma part of the truth. "We're not sure where the baron is at the moment, so I'm caring for his dog until he returns."

"Lord Beresford is missing?" Gemma's eyes widened.

"We don't have confirmation of that," Harriet said.

"But no one knows where he is?"

"Not exactly," Harriet said, intensely uneasy. "But I'm sure the police will find him soon."

"The police are involved?"

Oops.

"I'm sure he'll turn up soon," Harriet said. "And when he does, we'll have his dog waiting for him."

"That's very curious, isn't it? For him to vanish like that and leave his dog behind?"

Harriet could feel the conversation starting to spin out of control. "I probably shouldn't have said anything. You won't write about it, will you? I'm not sure it's supposed to be a public story."

Gemma paused for a moment, gazing at Harriet. She blinked, and a strange expression passed over her face. But finally she said, "Not if you don't want me to."

Harriet let out a breath. "Thank you. I don't know if I was supposed to say anything or not."

"No problem." Gemma pushed her empty glass aside. "But in any case, this has been a lovely time. Lucky we found each other, isn't it? I'd like to get together with you again."

"Absolutely." Harriet was glad she wasn't the only one who had enjoyed their meeting.

"Lovely. In that case, I'll settle the bill, and we'll be in touch shortly."

"That sounds wonderful. Let me know if you need anything more for your story."

Gemma smiled. "I will."

As Harriet stepped out of the pub, she found herself wondering if she'd found a new friend.

CHAPTER SEVEN

Back in the Land Rover, Harriet made her way toward Polly's house. Polly lived in Upper Bay, which wasn't all that big, but Harriet still got confused as she tried to navigate the narrow streets. Eventually, she pulled up in front of Polly's family home, a semi-detached brick cottage with a garden full of blooms in front. There were several cars parked in the driveway, so Harriet parked on the street and took the sidewalk to the front door. She rang the doorbell, and Coleridge barked from somewhere inside.

"Hello," Polly said, opening the door. She had changed into jeans and a pretty blouse, her hair was in an updo, and she'd used eyeliner and mascara. Coleridge appeared at her side, and Harriet held out her hand. Coleridge wagged his tail in recognition. "How was the interview?"

"I think it went well. You look very nice."

"Thank you." Polly held the door open and gestured for her to step inside. "First date. You know how it is."

Harriet smiled, though in truth she hadn't been on a first date in many years.

Behind Polly, someone in a recliner watched the news, and the smell of cooking meat and onions floated toward her. Harriet hadn't realized how hungry she was.

"Was everything okay?" Harriet asked, reaching out to pat Coleridge's head.

"Of course. We had a good time, didn't we, Coleridge?"

The dog continued to wag his tail. Polly picked up the leash from a small table in the entryway, clipped it onto the dog's collar, and handed it to Harriet.

"This is quite a posh collar, isn't it?" Polly said, raising an eyebrow. "Coleridge was scratching at it, so I adjusted it and saw that it's from Daisy. Probably Daisy Lyons, the breeder."

Harriet nodded. "I saw that Coleridge came from Lyons Breeders. But who is Daisy?"

"Well, she's a respected breeder, for one thing," Polly said. "Coleridge is one of hers. But more to the point, I always got the impression she's a friend of Liam Beresford. A *good* friend, if you know what I mean."

"Like a girlfriend?"

"I don't know that for sure, but I got to talking to him the first time he brought Coleridge in for his shots when he was a puppy. I was in the room when Liam told your grandad that Coleridge had been a gift from Daisy, who thought the dog would keep him from being lonely."

"That's quite a gift."

"That's what I thought. As soon as your grandfather left the room, I started chatting with Lord Beresford to see if I could find out what was what."

In the short time she'd known Polly, Harriet had discovered the young woman was quite good at chatting people up. She put people at ease, and people told her things they might not tell others. The previous week, Harriet had seen her work her magic on the owner of a Maltipoo with a stomachache. The owner reluctantly admitted that he'd fed the dog ice cream because it was so warm out.

But from what Harriet had heard, Lord Beresford was famously private. Had Polly gotten him to open up?

"What did he tell you?"

"I started chatting about how I'd heard Daisy had a good reputation as a breeder—which she does. But she's also distantly related to the royal family, so I was really trying to find out more about that."

"How distantly?"

"Second cousins twice removed or something like that. Still, it's closer than I've ever gotten to royalty. Anyway, I asked Lord Beresford about Daisy Lyons, and he said he'd known Daisy for years and that they'd even dated for a while when they were younger. Only he didn't use the word 'dated.' He said they'd been sweet on each other. I asked what happened, and he told me it wasn't meant to be but they'd reunited in recent years. He didn't come out and say it, but I assumed it had to do with the fact that they're both widowed and can be together again."

"So are they? Together again, I mean?"

Polly wrinkled her nose. "Your guess is as good as mine. Even I didn't have the guts to ask him that directly. 'Now that your wife is dead, did you go for it?' sounds kind of heartless. But the way he said it, I couldn't help but think there was something there."

Harriet wished they had a definite answer for her own curiosity, but it probably didn't matter anyway. The baron's love life wasn't any of her business.

Unless Daisy somehow knew where he'd gone. By all accounts, Lord Beresford was something of a loner, a recluse. Aunt Jinny had said that Grandad had been one of his few friends. But what if he had another friend, someone who might know where he'd gone?

He might very well be at the bottom of the bay. It was a grisly thought, but weren't the police boats out there right now, trying to either confirm or disprove that?

But even if he'd slipped off the crumbling cliff and fallen to his death, that didn't explain the disarray in his study. And it also didn't explain the curly-haired man lurking around Harriet's house and possibly trying to dognap Coleridge. How had Lord Beresford's jacket, which he'd presumably been wearing at the time of his fall, ended up off him and hanging on the driftwood? Why hadn't they found any other trace of him? In some ways, the cliff theory made sense, but in other ways, it brought up more questions than it answered. What if he hadn't fallen and they missed finding him because they were only searching in one place?

"Anyway, I've got to run. I'm due at the pub," Polly said.

"Thank you so much for watching Coleridge for me," Harriet said.

"No problem. He's a sweetie, isn't he?" Polly patted the dog's head, and Harriet led him out to the Land Rover and helped him in. Polly hopped into her little car and drove off, waving.

Harriet headed home, wondering about Daisy Lyons. Could she be the missing piece they needed to figure out what had happened to the baron?

At home, Harriet made herself dinner—chicken and a simple salad— and then took Coleridge on a walk before settling in for the night, but she had a hard time relaxing enough to go to bed. She was unsettled. Every creak and groan of the old house made her think someone was trying to break in, though Coleridge slept peacefully on the rug.

She kept thinking about the missing baron and about the fact that DI McCormick seemed to think Harriet had something to do with it, and about the man who had shown up at the house and fled twice. She thought about the broken cliff and about the scene of a scuffle in Liam Beresford's study and about Daisy Lyons, Coleridge's breeder and the baron's possible sweetheart.

She drank a cup of herbal tea, trying to relax. When that didn't work, she got up and grabbed her laptop. She opened a browser and typed in the name *Daisy Lyons*. That brought up thousands of results, so she added *Yorkshire* to the search terms. The first link that came up was a website for Lyons Breeders. Harriet scrolled through, momentarily distracted by the photos of bloodhound puppies who hadn't grown into their ears yet, but then she refocused and clicked on the About Us tab.

The page featured a picture of a tall, slender woman with gray hair wearing a blazer and Wellington boots. A few paragraphs of text described how she'd always loved bloodhounds. She'd grown up showing them and had been breeding them for nearly two decades. There was no personal information on the site besides an address and a phone number. The address was in Thornton-le-Dale, a small village in North Yorkshire.

She went back to the main search page and sorted through links for anything that might tell her more about Daisy Lyons personally rather than professionally. She found a few mentions of her on boards for local charities and on several pages of results for dog shows. Daisy had shown dogs several times at Crufts, which appeared to be the British equivalent of the Westminster Kennel Club Dog Show.

Halfway down the results, she came across an obituary in the *Times of London* for a Charles Lyons. She clicked on that and saw that it had been run two years ago, announcing the death of Charles Andrew Lyons of Yorkshire, a businessman and farmer, who was survived by his wife, Daisy, and their daughter, Emmaline. He must have been reasonably important if his obituary had ended up in the *Times*. But none of this got her any closer to finding out whether Daisy knew anything about Liam's disappearance.

But Daisy would be able to answer an important question. She would be able to confirm if Coleridge was a purebred bloodhound. If he was, that would lend credence to Harriet's suspicion that someone was trying to take Coleridge because of his monetary value.

Harriet thought for a moment, unsure what to do or how to phrase her question. Then, finally, she started an email to Daisy using the contact form on her website.

> *Ms. Lyons,*
>
> *My name is Harriet Bailey. I'm the new veterinarian in White Church Bay, having taken over the practice from my grandfather, Harold Bailey. I'm currently caring for a dog I think you know—Coleridge, owned by Lord Liam Beresford. He's a beautiful dog and a wonderful houseguest. I have a few questions about the dog and his owner, and I wondered if you might have a moment to discuss.*
>
> *Best wishes,*
>
> *Harriet*

She hoped Daisy would respond. For now, though, she was pretty sure she'd done as much as she could.

She thought for a moment. What about Liam's late wife? Who had she been, and why had Liam married her instead of Daisy? Mrs. Lewis had said her name was Beatrice.

Harriet opened a new browser window and searched the name *Beatrice Beresford*. She had an obituary in the *Times* as well.

The Baroness Beatrice Hart Beresford passed away on August 3, 2015, after a long battle with cancer. Beatrice was born July 17, 1962, in Birmingham, the daughter of Nolan Hart, the owner of Hart Shipping Company. She attended Institut Le Rosey in Switzerland before returning to the UK to attend Balliol College, Oxford. She married Lord Liam Beresford of White Church Bay, Yorkshire, in 1985, and had two children. She was a great lover of horses and spent most of her days riding. She is survived by her husband, Liam, the Baron of Beresford, and her children, Edward, the future Lord Beresford, and Stuart.

Poor Stuart. His name seemed so short and inconsequential compared to his brother's. It must be hard to be the second born, knowing everything went to the older brother.

A photo accompanied the obituary, showing the four family members in front of Beresford Manor. She studied Lord Beresford's face, realizing it was the first time she had ever seen him. It was a strange sensation, considering how her life had revolved around him over the past couple of days. He was tall, with broad shoulders, high cheekbones, a widow's peak, and a dimpled chin. She couldn't tell how old the photo was, but the sons seemed to be in their late teens or early twenties in this photograph, and they had to be several years older than that now.

That was interesting enough, but it didn't tell her much she hadn't already known. She clicked around online, searching for any additional information about Beatrice but soon grew frustrated. Even if she knew more about the baron's late wife, how did that get her any closer to finding out what had happened to him?

What about his sons? Did they know anything? Harriet opened another browser window and typed in the name *Edward Beresford*. She found an article in the *Times of London* that quoted him talking about a new development that would replace some existing houses in a less fashionable London neighborhood with "a more walkable, sustainable growth plan." The article strongly suggested that this mostly involved eliminating low-income housing and replacing it with more profitable commercial development. To Harriet, the article didn't cast the future Lord Beresford in a great light, but she was far from an expert on the topic.

She also found his name in a list of results of horse shows from many years ago. She remembered that Mrs. Lewis had said the stables at Beresford Manor had been empty since Beatrice passed. But there were horses once, and Edward had apparently been quite good at show jumping when he was younger.

She clicked around some more and found a social media account for him. There were pictures of a man with reddish hair and a ruddy complexion posing with a stunning woman with long brown hair. They had three teenage children, two boys and a girl, and seemed to spend a lot of time traveling and hanging around on boats.

She clicked back to the main search page and started a search for *Stuart Beresford*. Liam's younger son was a barrister—a lawyer—in Toronto. He had brown hair, high cheekbones, and a strong chin, and wore a tailored suit in the picture on the website of his law firm. She could see from his social media page that he was married to a blond woman, and they had a daughter. The family seemed to spend a lot of time camping and hiking. Stuart was also a carpenter, with a website dedicated to showcasing the bespoke furniture and household items he made from reclaimed wood. It was beautiful but pricey.

Neither son mentioned anything about a missing father on their social media. Did they even know? Surely the police had contacted them. But regardless of whether they knew anything, they hadn't posted about it publicly.

She wasn't sure why she was so intrigued by all this. The police were investigating the baron's disappearance. Whatever the truth was, they would find it. They hardly needed the help of a veterinarian from another country who had merely stumbled upon the situation.

Yet she couldn't help trying to find out more. She didn't know if it was because she'd seen the mess in the study before the police had, or if it was because Coleridge—Lord Beresford's dearest companion, by all accounts—was staying with her, or because she had the distinct impression that the police considered her a suspect and she wanted to clear her name. Perhaps it was a little bit of all those things.

Regardless, she wasn't about to let it go.

CHAPTER EIGHT

Harriet slept poorly and woke early on Wednesday morning. She let Coleridge and Maxwell out while she brewed coffee and picked up the paper, which had been delivered just a few minutes before. Harriet scanned the headlines while the dogs ran around the yard.

One grabbed her attention. POLICE SEARCH FOR MISSING BARON. She read the article quickly.

> Lord Liam Beresford has been reported missing, last seen Friday, and the police are searching for any clues to his whereabouts. Searches of Beresford Manor have turned up few clues, sources report, though the baron's dog was found roaming the village, leading to suspicion that foul play might be involved. Local authorities declined to comment on the case. Anyone with information about his whereabouts should contact the White Church Bay police.

So it had made the paper then. But there was no byline attached to the short piece, which was in a section that reported on local police activity.

For a moment, Harriet thought about Gemma. Was there any chance she'd written the article? But she'd said she wouldn't print what Harriet had told her, and she'd given Harriet no reason not to trust her.

She brought the dogs in and spent some time reading about David's exploits as Saul pursued the future king through the countryside. Coleridge lay next to her on the couch, his head in her lap. After her reading, she asked the Lord to bless her day, those she came in contact with, and her friends and family back home. As she stroked Coleridge's head, she asked for Liam Beresford to come home safely.

Then she checked her email and was delighted to find a response from Daisy Lyons. Harriet opened it.

> *Harriet,*
>
> *Your late grandfather was a dear man, and I was so sorry to hear of his passing. However, I am delighted to make your acquaintance. I know Coleridge well and would be happy to answer questions about my dear friend Lord Beresford. Would you like to come around and see the new litter I have? Puppies can make any appointment a delight, and it's always good for breeders and vets to network with each other. If you have some time Thursday or Friday, I would welcome a visit. Please let me know.*
>
> *Yours,*
>
> *Daisy Lyons*

Harriet realized she was smiling. Daisy would be able to confirm Coleridge's pedigree, and maybe she would even know something about Lord Beresford's whereabouts. Besides, Daisy was right that it made sense for the local vet to know the dog breeders in the area. She consulted her work calendar and saw that she was due to vaccinate some sheep on a farm near Daisy's home on Thursday morning.

She wrote back, asking Daisy if a visit around eleven o'clock would work.

After she'd fed the animals and herself, she headed to the clinic with them in tow. Her first appointment was out in the field, a set of routine shots for the horses on a nearby farm, and she needed to gather the injections.

"Good morning," Polly said from behind the desk. "Hi, Coleridge. Nice to see you're getting along well with Maxwell and Charlie."

He wagged his tail. Maxwell wheeled his way over to Polly to say hello. Charlie jumped up on the counter and pretended she couldn't see or hear anything that was going on.

"Good morning," Harriet said. "You're here early."

"I wanted to make sure I didn't fall behind on filing, since I'm leaving early on Friday."

"I appreciate your dedication. Did you have a nice time last night?" Harriet asked.

"It was okay," Polly said. "I don't know if there'll be a second date, but he was nice enough."

"I'm sorry about that." Dating could be so awkward. Harriet didn't know how Polly could enjoy it as much as she did.

"Don't be. It's always worth getting to know someone new, isn't it? I always say yes if someone asks, because you never know."

"That's a good attitude." It also sounded exhausting, which probably confirmed that Harriet wasn't ready to get back into it yet.

"There's not much going on around here anyway. At least this way I get to meet some new people," Polly said. "You're headed over to the Ridgeways' farm first thing, right?"

"Yes, for their horses' annual physical and shots."

"They'll want you to check something else once you're there," Polly said with a chuckle. "The sheep, or the cows, or a dog. One time there was a chicken emergency. Doc Bailey always budgeted an extra hour at their place because it inevitably took longer than he'd expected. I've blocked off the whole morning to be on the safe side."

"A chicken emergency?"

"One of the chickens swallowed a coin."

"That would do it." Chickens would eat anything, and the metal in coins was toxic to their systems.

"Yeah, so plan to be there a while."

"Thank you." Harriet would be lost without Polly and her experience at the clinic. "In that case, I'll take more supplies than I originally planned to." She was hopeful she could still make it to Beresford Manor by eleven to meet Mrs. Lewis.

"I'll be catching up on billing, but let me know if you need me to do anything else while you're out."

"How would you feel about looking after Coleridge until I get back?"

"We'll have a grand time, won't we, boy?" Polly cooed at the dog, who thumped his tail on the floor.

"Thank you. I'll see you later." Harriet loaded up her bag and set out. Even though she was still getting used to driving on the left side of the road, she loved cruising through the countryside. The rolling hills were dotted with scrubby trees, grazing sheep, and rocky outcroppings. The stark beauty of the place was almost hypnotic.

She found the farm easily enough. True to Polly's prediction, as soon as she'd finished giving the horses their shots, Pete Ridgeway asked her to take a look at a lamb that was doing poorly, then an alpaca with a sore foot.

Fortunately, both cases were easy to treat. She said goodbye to the grateful farmer and headed to Beresford Manor to meet Mrs. Lewis.

It really is impressive, she reflected as she drove up the long driveway. It was hard to believe this was a private residence and that one man lived in this enormous old house all alone.

She parked next to Mrs. Lewis's car in the round section of the driveway, noting that the Bentley was still in the same spot, and rang the doorbell. She tried to imagine what it must have been like to arrive at this house by carriage and be greeted by a butler in tails. Surely that must have happened at some point in the house's history.

"Hello, Harriet," Mrs. Lewis said, pulling the heavy front door open. There were dark circles under her eyes, and her mouth was tight with concern. "Come on in. How are you?"

"I'm fine. How are you?"

"A bit anxious, if you want to know the truth." Mrs. Lewis ushered Harriet inside.

Harriet stepped into the great hall and took it all in once again. The soaring ceiling, the marble floors, the elaborately carved mahogany staircase, the paneled walls. It was all designed to impress, and it did the job.

"I was down in the village earlier," Mrs. Lewis continued. "And I heard they were dragging the bay for the lord's body. I can't—I hope—" She broke off and pressed her fingertips to her trembling lips.

Harriet had heard much about the British stiff upper lip, but she could see that Mrs. Lewis fought back tears. Harriet sincerely hoped Lord Beresford was found alive, but Mrs. Lewis had known and worked for him for years, and she must be feeling this on a completely different level.

"They haven't found anything yet, at least not that I've heard," Harriet said. "It's entirely possible they won't."

"Susan at the market said the cliff fell away and they found something of his below, on the beach. Susan didn't know what it was, but she told me you were the one who found it."

"With my aunt Jinny," Harriet said. "We walked Coleridge Monday night, and he led us to where the cliff had given way. Below we saw a jacket that my aunt said belonged to Lord Beresford. It was caught on a piece of driftwood."

"What did it look like?" Mrs. Lewis asked.

"Black-and-gray houndstooth."

"The houndstooth jacket?" Mrs. Lewis brightened at that. What was so exciting about houndstooth? "The knee-length one?"

"I don't know," Harriet said. "I suppose so. I didn't see it up close. Aunt Jinny said she recognized it as his."

"It is his." Mrs. Lewis nodded. "Or it was. The thing is, I took that jacket to the charity shop a few weeks back."

"You did?"

"He'd had it for so long it was worn right through in some places. Peter sent him a nice new light wool coat last Christmas, perfect for chilly evening walks along the cliffs. Last month I finally convinced Lord Beresford it was time to let go of the houndstooth one."

"Wait. So the coat we found wasn't his?"

"Not anymore." Mrs. Lewis smiled, and the heaviness seemed to have gone out of her eyes. "So if that's why they think he might be at the bottom of the bay, they may be searching in the wrong place."

"Really?" Harriet felt her heart grow lighter. This was wonderful news.

"Really." Mrs. Lewis laughed. "Thank goodness. I have to call DC Worthington and let him know."

"Yes, please do."

"Let me get that medication for you, and then I'll call the station." Her countenance was considerably brighter than it had been when Harriet first arrived. "Follow me."

Harriet admired her surroundings as she followed Mrs. Lewis toward the parlor. The woodwork on the walls was incredible, and the paintings in the spaces on the coffered ceilings were works of art.

"This place is gorgeous."

"It's a beautiful house, isn't it? Been in the lord's family for nearly four centuries. Of course, it's changed a lot in that time, but it's still pretty nice, don't you think?"

"I would say that's an understatement," Harriet said with a laugh.

"I'm sorry I forgot the medicine," Mrs. Lewis said. "I was so scattered on Monday that I didn't know my right from my left. I'm surprised I even gave you the right food and leash."

"You'd had quite a shock," Harriet said. "It would have thrown anyone off."

"You're right, of course," Mrs. Lewis said. "Plus, caring for Coleridge was never one of my duties. I take care of the house and cook, but Lord Beresford cares for the dog himself."

"I understand," Harriet said. "It must be quite an undertaking, managing such a large house. Do you do it by yourself?"

"Yes. The inside, anyway. There are gardeners who maintain the grounds. The stables haven't been used for years, so they don't have to worry about that. And the workers' cottages that used to be part of the property were sold off a long time ago, so that makes things easier. But I keep the house itself in order. It's a big job." She sounded quite proud, and Harriet couldn't blame her. It was impressive that one person could do it all. "Of course, most of the house isn't used these days, so that helps. Most of the bedrooms are shut up, as well as the formal entertaining spaces. Lord Beresford is a rather neat man, so he's not hard to clean up after."

"And you have your own key?" Harriet followed her into the parlor, once again amazed by the high ceilings and large fireplace.

"Yes. I can come and go as needed without disturbing Lord Beresford."

"Who else has a key to the house?"

"That's a good question. The gardeners don't. Maybe his solicitor? I'm not sure. Why?" Mrs. Lewis asked. "You don't think someone came in and hurt him, do you?"

"I'm just trying to get a more complete picture," Harriet said. "I can't stop thinking about the missing baron, and the more we're able to put things together, the more likely it is that we'll find him."

"I haven't stopped thinking about him either," Mrs. Lewis said.

"What about members of the family? Doesn't the baron have two sons?" Harriet asked as they walked past the door to the study. The rug had been straightened, the table righted, and the broken glass cleared away. The laptop that had been on the desk was gone.

"That's right." The sound of their footsteps disappeared into the soft pile of the huge wool rug in the library. "Edward lives in London, and Stuart's in Toronto. They may have keys—they grew up here, after all—but they never come around these days. And even if they did, they wouldn't need a key. Their father would let them in."

"That's a shame, that they don't come and see their father more often. Especially Edward, who's relatively local."

"It is."

"Do you think there's any chance one of them came to visit their father last weekend?"

Harriet didn't know for sure that someone else had been here before Lord Beresford disappeared, but the signs of the scuffle in the study made her wonder. She supposed it was possible that he'd disturbed the rug on his own, that he'd knocked over the table and thrown the decanter at the wall, and added drops of blood to the glass. But it would make a lot more sense if someone had been in the study with him and there'd been an argument of some kind. If Lord Beresford's relationship with his sons was rocky, that could give a possible explanation for who might have been visiting.

But all Mrs. Lewis said about it was, "They don't come by very often."

Harriet waited for her to elaborate but soon gave up that idea. She supposed it was a good thing that the housekeeper wasn't inclined to gossip about her employer.

So she decided to explore another theory. "Is there anyone who might have been particularly interested in Coleridge?" Maybe whoever had been there had come for Coleridge in the first place, and when Lord Beresford wouldn't sell him, things had gotten violent. That could explain the strange man who kept appearing at Cobble Hill Farm.

"Not that I know of," Mrs. Lewis said. "Truth be told, your grandfather was the only one who ever paid much attention to the dog, aside from Lord Beresford himself."

"You never saw anyone hanging around, trying to get close to the dog?"

"No." Mrs. Lewis raised an eyebrow at her. "Why would anyone want to do that?"

Harriet didn't bother to explain that Coleridge was likely valuable. Instead, she asked, "Have you ever heard of a Daisy Lyons?"

"Of course," Mrs. Lewis said. "She's a friend of Lord Beresford. She's the breeder who gave him Coleridge. You don't think she wanted him to return the dog, do you?"

"I don't know," Harriet said. "It doesn't seem especially likely, but I don't really know anything about her."

"Those two are such friends that I imagine if she wanted Coleridge back, all she'd need to do is ask. She's the one who finally wore Lord Beresford down in the first place." She said the last part with a laugh.

"What do you mean, wore him down?"

"I'd been telling him for years he should get a dog. It wasn't right, him rattling around in this big old house all by himself. I tried to encourage him to get a dog, or even a cat, just to have something else around, you know? He said he was surrounded by his ancestors and never felt alone here."

"What did he mean by that?" Harriet asked.

"Somehow, being here in this house that's been passed down from his father, and his father, and his father—well, I think it makes him feel secure, if that makes sense. More connected to those who came before him."

Harriet supposed it did, in a strange way. She couldn't imagine living in a house that had been in her family for that long, but she supposed it could feel comforting.

"Anyway, he didn't listen to me, but one day Daisy showed up with the puppy and said it was his now, and that was that. Lord Beresford has a dog, and it was the best thing that happened to him in a long time."

"What do you make of their relationship?" Harriet asked as they reached the back of the house.

"Daisy and the lord's?" Mrs. Lewis clarified. "I couldn't say. She comes around sometimes. She's one of the few who does, so that's something."

"Is there any chance she came to see him last weekend?"

"I can't say one way or the other, but I can't see her causing that mess in the study," she said. "Daisy is a real lady. Whatever happened in there, Daisy didn't throw that decanter."

That didn't mean Liam hadn't though. Maybe they'd gotten into a fight. Maybe there was more to their relationship than friendship. Anything was possible.

"Do you think Lord Beresford could have been the one to throw the decanter?"

Mrs. Lewis stepped into the kitchen and flipped on the overhead light. She started opening cabinets. "That's strange. I wonder if he moved it."

"The medicine?"

"That's right. It's usually kept here. I wonder where it is."

How strange. Had Lord Beresford taken it with him when he'd gone wherever he'd gone? Was the missing medicine a mere coincidence—or a clue?

CHAPTER NINE

W ell, fortunately, I can get more for him," Harriet assured her.

"I'm glad of that. I just wish I knew where it went." Mrs. Lewis rose up on her toes, peering toward the back of the cabinet.

Harriet checked the time and realized that if she wanted to ask Mrs. Lewis any other questions, she'd better do it sooner rather than later.

"Do you know anything about a group called End Peerage Now?" Harriet asked. The police officers must think there was a possibility the group was connected to the baron's disappearance, since they'd asked her about it. She wondered what Mrs. Lewis thought of them.

Mrs. Lewis closed the cabinet door. "Nasty bunch that always stirs up trouble. Just sour grapes, if you ask me. I wasn't born into nobility, but I don't spend all my time going around complaining about it, do I?"

"I read that they sometimes harass members of the peerage. Has anything like that ever happened here?"

"Depends on what you call harassment, I suppose. They've never staged one of their protests here. I don't suppose Lord Beresford is ranked high enough for one of those. But we get the mail like everyone else."

"Anything in particular?"

"Near-weekly letters. You'd think they'd get sick of it after a while when they get no response, but they still come."

"What kind of letters? Could I see them?"

Mrs. Lewis narrowed her eyes.

"I'm sorry. That's probably a strange request. I recently learned about this group," Harriet said. "And I was curious about them. I read about their protests, but I didn't realize they sent mail as well."

"I collect the mail for Lord Beresford when I'm here, and I pull their mail out and put it with the junk mail so Lord Beresford doesn't see it. It would upset him, and he doesn't need that. But I suppose it wouldn't hurt to show you."

She led Harriet into a hallway. Several large closets—pantries, she supposed, designed to store goods to feed a house full of family and servants—were along one side, and on the other side, Mrs. Lewis led her into a small room that was set up as an office. A desk took up much of the room. Filing cabinets lined the walls, and a stack of mail sat in a wire basket, apparently waiting to be filed.

"Most of what I do is cleaning and cooking, but I also file the bills, order groceries, that kind of thing," she explained, ushering Harriet inside. "This room has always belonged to the housekeeper, so I thought it was the perfect space for all this. Back in the day, there was a live-in housekeeper, but with the lord by himself now, I can handle what needs to be done." She picked up the stack of mail and sorted through it. "Here it is." She took an envelope out of the stack and handed it to Harriet. "I gave the others I hadn't thrown out to the police, but this one came today. You can tell who it's from because they all look the same. Plain white envelope, no return address, handwriting like a child's."

The name *Liam Beresford*—not Lord Beresford—was written in blue ink, along with the address. Mrs. Lewis was right. The handwriting was juvenile. Harriet flipped the envelope over and saw that it was still sealed.

"May I open it?" she asked.

"Sure. They're all the same." Mrs. Lewis offered her a letter opener from the desk.

Harriet sliced open the envelope, took out the letter, and unfolded it. It looked like it had been printed from a computer, and there was no signature at the bottom.

> *Liam Beresford:*
> *Given the undeniable and unforgivable inequities in our society, it is inexcusable that some continue to live like kings with inherited titles and lands while others starve. You have done nothing to earn the privilege of this title and bring nothing of value to society with it. Change is coming, and it will not be easy for those who refuse to give up the old ways of oppression and suppression. Relinquish your title and lands, and you will be spared when the revolution comes.*

"Whoa." Harriet hadn't expected it to be quite so menacing. "That's a direct threat."

"I worried about them at first. But they come about once a week, and there's not much to be done. The police don't know who's sending them and can't devote much manpower to finding out unless something actually happens."

"What if it does?"

Mrs. Lewis's mouth pinched at the corners. "When they first started coming, I urged Lord Beresford to get private security, but he wouldn't hear of it. Said people had always wanted to get rid of peerage, and they had never succeeded, so why worry about it now. I couldn't convince him."

"But what if something *has* happened?"

"That's why I gave the others to the police," Mrs. Lewis said. "They're going to try to trace them, though they didn't have much luck before. I hope that whatever has happened to the baron doesn't involve these loonies."

"I completely agree. When did they first start arriving?"

"Five years or so ago. It was right before my Marian got married, I remember that. I had to talk with the police when I was supposed to be helping her pick out napkins for the reception."

Harriet assumed Marian was Mrs. Lewis's daughter. She flipped the envelope over again. "I'm glad the police are digging into this."

According to the postmark, it had been mailed from Leeds, a large city about two hours away from White Church Bay. Hopefully, the police would find whoever had sent it. Then, she realized that if this letter did have anything to do with the baron's disappearance, there might be fingerprints on it, and now she'd added her own fingerprints all over it as well. She set the envelope down quickly.

Mrs. Lewis sorted through the rest of the mail. She'd set aside what looked like two utility bills and was gazing at a colorful brochure. The front had a picture of a castle perched on a hill.

"Another travel brochure," she said, setting the pamphlet on the desk. "I don't know why Canterbury Travel seems to think Lord

Beresford wants to go to Spain—or anywhere else for that matter. He never goes on holiday."

"Has he gotten brochures like that before?"

"For the past three months or so, it's been constant. I'm about to call Brigitte and tell her to stop wasting paper and my time. He's never going to go on a holiday to Spain."

"Did he get travel brochures before that?" Harriet asked. It seemed odd that they would suddenly start arriving without reason.

"No," Mrs. Lewis said. "Everyone knows he never goes anywhere. I don't know what made Brigitte think now would be the perfect time and that Spain is the place that would suddenly make him pack his bags." She flipped open the brochure. Harriet could see a photo of a sandy beach on the back. "Though I will say, it is pretty. If I could swing it, I'd go myself."

Wasn't that the purpose of a travel brochure, to make you think about how nice it would be to visit?

Harriet thought for a moment and had an idea that would probably sound silly. But it wouldn't hurt to ask. "Is there any chance he actually did go on a trip?"

"To Spain? Not likely."

"But is it possible? If not to Spain, then somewhere else?"

"If Lord Beresford had a trip planned, he would have told me, wouldn't he?" Mrs. Lewis sounded certain. "I'm here four days a week, managing his meals and such. He didn't say anything about not laying in food for the week as normal."

"Maybe it was a spur-of-the-moment trip?"

"To Spain?"

Harriet had never been on a spur-of-the-moment international trip personally, but she didn't know what rich people did. And to be fair, her theory didn't explain why he'd left his dog. "To anywhere."

"His car is here. Not that he would drive to Spain, obviously," Mrs. Lewis amended. "But he would probably drive to the airport. And that wouldn't explain the evidence of a fight in the study. Besides, he would have lined up someone to care for Coleridge, even at the last minute. He knows you run a kennel, and he loves that dog. He'd never let run him free through the streets while he took off on holiday."

That was all true enough. But Harriet couldn't let go of the idea without checking on the facts rather than supposition. What if he hadn't taken off to leave the dog running free? Perhaps he had made arrangements for Coleridge. The missing medication gave credence to that possibility. But then again, what arrangements could he have made? Coleridge was a patient at her clinic, so wouldn't he have boarded the dog with her? Someone who loved his dog as much as Lord Beresford loved his would have wanted to trust whoever watched Coleridge, especially with his medical condition.

"Does Lord Beresford have luggage?"

"Yes," she said. "There are four suitcases in the storage room. Well, technically, it's a bedroom, but it's one of the rooms in the west wing that's never used. Now it's more like a big closet."

"Is it worth checking to see if any of them are missing?"

Mrs. Lewis pressed her lips together. Obviously, she didn't think there was any chance the baron had taken a suitcase and gone on vacation. And she was probably right. Mrs. Lewis certainly knew Lord Beresford's habits better than Harriet did, and she was also right that the other factors she'd mentioned indicated that he hadn't simply gone away on a spur-of-the-moment trip.

Harriet didn't want to pry. She was just the local vet, not the police. Still, she couldn't understand why Mrs. Lewis would not at least explore the possibility, if only to cross it off the list entirely. "At least then you'd know for sure?"

Mrs. Lewis sighed. "All right. I'll go check. Why don't you wait in the library?" She led Harriet to the room then said, "I'll be back shortly."

Harriet gazed around the library with its heavy draperies, its leather-clad club chairs, and its floor-to-ceiling bookshelves, lined with leather-bound volumes. It was a booklover's dream.

She walked to the closest wall and studied the spines of the books, admiring a collection of Shakespeare's works. *Hamlet, As You Like It, A Midsummer Night's Dream*. Maybe now that she lived in England, she should go to London and see a production at the Globe Theatre.

On the next shelf was an illustrated version of Chaucer's *The Canterbury Tales* next to a beautiful volume of Milton's *Paradise Lost*. Below that, there were slim books—the collected poems of Lord Byron, Alfred Lord Tennyson, John Keats, T.S. Eliot, William Wordsworth, and Samuel Taylor Coleridge.

The name Coleridge snagged her attention. Had Lord Beresford named his dog after a poet?

She slid the book, *Lyrical Ballads*, off the shelf and gently flipped through the pages. A good chunk of the book was taken up by one long poem called "The Rime of the Ancient Mariner." She hadn't read that poem since an introductory literature class in college. She remembered something about a sailor killing an albatross and bad things happening as a result. She'd never cared for any of the Romantic poets all that much, but she supposed the name made sense for a dog whose home was perched on a cliff overlooking a fishing village.

She closed the book gently and slid it back onto the shelf and then proceeded down the row, scanning the titles of books about history and science.

Then she came to a shelf that held a collection of framed family photos. She stepped closer to a wedding photo and recognized much-younger versions of the baron and Beatrice in front of White Church.

There were formal school portraits of Edward and Stuart. One appeared to be a framed photograph of the whole family standing in front of the Colosseum in Rome. It had been taken several decades before, judging by the age of the children and the soft yellowish tinge in the photo. So the baron hadn't always stayed close to home. She wondered what had changed.

Then she found even older photos. There was one of a child wearing shorts, a sweater, and oxfords with knee-high socks, standing with a man and a woman. Harriet guessed the photo was of the baron and his parents. His father wore a gray suit and tie, while his mother had on an A-line dress with cap sleeves, her blond hair in a bouffant. The mother held a baby in her arms, probably Aunt Jinny's old friend Peter. The parents were in other photos as well, including several with another couple around the same age. One showed the four of them posed on a mountain in ski gear, and another had them in front of a large lake surrounded by rolling green hills.

Mrs. Lewis stepped back into the room. "Sorry, that took longer than I expected. I hope you weren't too bored."

"Not at all. I was looking at these old photos." Harriet gestured at the picture of the couple with the small boy and baby. "Is this the baron?"

Mrs. Lewis strode over and leaned in. "Yes, that's his lordship when he was small. He was cute, wasn't he?"

"He was."

"Those are his parents, of course, and there are other pictures of them with friends of the family. Anyway, those photos have been there for as long as I've worked here, so I don't know who placed them. Likely not Lord Beresford. He's not sentimental like that. All I know for sure is that the frames attract dust."

"I'm sure. Did you find anything?"

Mrs. Lewis frowned. "It's the strangest thing. I went to the room where the suitcases are kept. There should be two big ones and two small ones. The late missus was very particular about them. I've dusted them so many times."

Harriet waited, not sure where she was going with this.

"But when I looked just now, there were only three suitcases. One of the large ones is missing."

CHAPTER TEN

It took Harriet a moment to process what this meant.

"You mean Lord Beresford went on a trip after all?"

"I suppose so," Mrs. Lewis said, though she didn't look convinced. "I doubt whoever he quarreled with went up and took a suitcase."

"No, that doesn't seem likely," Harriet said. She could see the housekeeper was as stunned as she was. "Where do you think he went?" Could Lord Beresford have gone to Spain? Or to London or Canada to visit one of his sons?

"I have no idea," Mrs. Lewis said. "It doesn't make sense."

"I wonder if we should call Edward or Stuart," Harriet suggested. "I imagine the police have already been in touch with them, but still."

Mrs. Lewis nodded. "The police told me they would do so. I gave them both boys' numbers."

"What about the baron's passport?" Harriet asked. "Is that still here?"

"I don't know. He keeps it in the safe in his study, and I don't have access to that."

That was too bad. At least that would tell them whether he'd gone abroad or not.

"I suppose I should let the police know about this," Mrs. Lewis said.

"Yes, I think that makes sense," Harriet said. It seemed to be increasingly likely that Liam had left of his own accord, given the revelation about the jacket and the missing suitcase. But if that was true, where had he gone, and why hadn't he told anyone? And what about Coleridge? What about the mess in the study? Even if he had left on purpose, some things still didn't add up.

"I'll do that now."

"Thank you. I should get going," Harriet said.

"I'll walk you up front," Mrs. Lewis said.

Harriet appreciated the offer, as she was nervous that she'd get lost in the grand house. "I do hope they find him soon," she said as she stepped out the front door at last.

"I hope so too," Mrs. Lewis said. "I also hope I haven't raised a big fuss if all he's done is go on holiday."

"The circumstances are suspicious enough that I think it's good they're looking for him," Harriet assured her. "Please let me know if there's any way I can help."

"You already have, with that suitcase question, to say nothing of everything you're doing for Coleridge," Mrs. Lewis said. "Thank you again. I'll see you later."

She closed the big heavy door behind her, and Harriet walked to the Rover. She'd been gone longer than she intended, and she needed to get back in time for her afternoon appointments.

She drove through the rolling hills and pulled into the small lot in front of her house, glad to see Mrs. Winslow's car in front of the art gallery. The idea of opening her grandfather's space to the public again always warmed her heart. Mrs. Winslow had been a part-time docent at the gallery before Grandad passed, and Harriet was delighted when she volunteered to step back into the role again. It was one less thing she needed to worry about.

As Harriet climbed out of the car, her phone rang, and the name *Gemma Loughty* lit up the screen. Harriet swiped to answer. "Hello?"

"Hello, Harriet, it's Gemma. How are you?"

"I'm doing all right," Harriet said. "And you?"

"I'm good. Listen, I had a couple of follow-up questions to ask you. Would you mind meeting me again? It'd be fun to get to know more about you."

"Sure." Harriet felt a rush of delight. Gemma could have simply asked her the follow-up questions on the phone, but she wanted to hang out. Harriet hadn't simply imagined that they'd gotten along well. Gemma had felt it too. "When?"

"How about later today?"

"Sure. I have a few appointments this afternoon, but I should be done by four."

"Great. Why don't I meet you in the village? Maybe at that adorable tearoom?"

"The Happy Cup?" Harriet had seen the tearoom and bakery in the village. "That sounds great."

Polly greeted Harriet when she stepped inside, and pointed to where Maxwell and Coleridge slept side by side in the waiting area.

Harriet smiled. "That's so sweet."

"They've been inseparable all day," Polly said. "Anyway, your three o'clock canceled. Apparently, Horace the turtle is doing much better. So you only have a few appointments this afternoon."

"Great, on both counts. I have a meeting at four."

The afternoon passed swiftly, and soon it was time to close. Harriet didn't want to leave Coleridge alone with a potential dognapper on the loose, but she hated to impose on Polly again.

"Nonsense," Polly said at once when Harriet brought it up. "I'm happy to do it."

"Are you sure?" Harriet asked anxiously. "It would only be for an hour or so."

Polly waved her off. "Take as much time as you need. We'll have a good time together, won't we, boy?"

Coleridge thumped his tail on the floor.

So Harriet changed and headed into the village. She found Gemma waiting for her in the small tearoom. Gemma greeted Harriet, air-kissing both of her cheeks. "Hello, friend."

"Hello. This place is so cute. I can't believe I haven't been in here yet." A big bay window made up of many small panes let in plenty of light, and the light wood floors and bright white walls were complemented by tablecloths and paintings in soft shades of pink, butter yellow, and sage green.

"It is, isn't it?" Gemma had straightened her hair today, and it fell down her back. "Let's go grab something, and then we can have a chat."

Together they made their way to the counter. Harriet ordered a latte, and Gemma chose a pot of Earl Grey. Gemma insisted on paying for both drinks, ignoring Harriet's protest that she'd paid the previous day as well. She guessed the newspaper gave Gemma an expense budget for interviews. After all, she was on the clock. The woman behind the counter promised to bring out the drinks in a few minutes, and they chose a table.

"It's good to see you again," Gemma said as soon as they were seated.

"You as well."

"How's the dog?"

"Coleridge?"

"The one you had to rush off and take care of, who belongs to the missing baron."

"He's fine," Harriet said.

"What about the baron?" Gemma asked. "Has he turned up yet?"

"Not yet," Harriet said. Gemma had said she wouldn't write about it, but Harriet had to ask. "Gemma, I saw a short article in the paper today about the missing baron. That wasn't you, was it?"

"That bit in the police blotter? No, that's someone else's beat."

Harriet had been pretty sure, but it still felt good to hear Gemma say it. "Okay, good." Then, just to make sure, she added, "So this is off the record, right?"

"Of course," Gemma assured her. "Totally off the record."

"Okay." She wouldn't report on it, so it should be okay to talk about it. Perhaps her new friend would have a perspective Harriet hadn't thought of. "He's still missing. For a while it seemed like there was a chance he'd fallen from the cliffs into the bay, but now it seems more likely he went on a trip without telling anyone."

Gemma's eyes widened. "A secret holiday? How exciting."

A woman appeared with Harriet's latte then set a pot of tea in a quilted cozy in front of Gemma, along with a teacup, a tiny bowl of sugar cubes, and a small pitcher of cream. It was all so cute that Harriet decided she would order that next time she visited the shop.

"I don't know if it's secret or exciting," Harriet said when the server left. "His housekeeper thought he wouldn't have gone on holiday, because he's something of a recluse, but his suitcase is missing."

Gemma poured rich, fragrant tea into her cup. "Does he have a secret girlfriend? Someone he ran away to meet?"

"I wouldn't know. There may be someone, but no one seems to be sure what their relationship is, or was."

"Well, there you go. Perhaps they ran off together."

"That's not likely. I've been in touch with her. I'm supposed to meet with her tomorrow morning. And what reason would they have to run away?"

"That does throw some water on that theory. Well, maybe that's not it." Gemma stirred cream into her tea then picked up the cup and sat back against her seat. "Okay, tell me about the cliff thing. What's that about?"

Harriet told Gemma about Coleridge sniffing at the fallen cliff, the jacket they'd found below, and the boats dragging the bay. "But I found out this afternoon the jacket doesn't even belong to Lord Beresford anymore," Harriet said. "The housekeeper donated it to the charity shop."

"So how did it wind up on the beach?" Gemma mused. "Did someone else fall off the cliff and into the bay? Or—*ooh*. Maybe the baron pushed whoever it was. That would explain why he left town so suddenly. He had to run before someone found out what he'd done"

Harriet opened her mouth to argue. Lord Beresford would never—

She closed her mouth just as suddenly as she'd opened it. She didn't know him well enough to make that assertion, or at all, really.

She had no idea what he'd do. And Gemma had a point. If he had left town, there must be a reason. Running away after committing a crime was an obvious motive. It could explain the scene in the study—he'd quarreled with someone, things turned physical, the decanter was thrown, and it somehow ended with Beresford pushing his rival too close to the edge of the crumbling cliff. It could also explain why he'd left suddenly, without giving word to Mrs. Lewis or making arrangements for Coleridge. He hadn't had time.

"That would be murder," Harriet breathed.

"Or manslaughter, if it was an accident," Gemma said. "But who else was involved? Is anyone else missing?"

"I don't know. I haven't heard of anyone." Harriet sipped her latte. "Is it too much of a coincidence that in this scenario the baron happens to push someone off the cliff who was wearing his old coat?"

"Maybe it's not a coincidence at all." Gemma's eyes widened. "Maybe he killed the person *because* they wore his old coat. Maybe there was something special about that coat, or about why they were wearing it. What if there was something in the coat pocket or even sewn into the lining, something valuable or incriminating, and he wanted it back? Maybe whoever it was bought that coat from the charity shop to spite Lord Beresford. The new owner might have even blackmailed him, or maybe Liam asked for it to be returned and the new owner refused. So a fight broke out in the study, and then the baron followed the new owner to the cliff specifically to push him off."

"That's a lot of maybes."

"So how would we find out if any of those maybes are true?" Gemma asked. She finished her first cup of tea and poured a second. "It's like an Agatha Christie novel, except it's real."

Harriet considered the question. "I guess we would need to find out who ended up with that coat."

"We could ask at the charity shop. Find out who bought it. Surely they would remember who bought a memorable coat like that." Gemma added sugar to her cup. "Then we need to figure out where he ran off to."

"*If* that's what happened," Harriet said. "And that's a pretty big *if.*"

"Of course," Gemma agreed. "We're just throwing out theories. It's one possibility."

"One I hope isn't true."

"Of course we hope this isn't really what happened. But it can't hurt to speculate. It could lead us to the truth."

"I suppose." Gemma had come up with a possibility Harriet hadn't thought of—and it seemed an obvious possibility, now that she'd mentioned it. "How about Spain?"

"Why Spain?"

"The housekeeper said he'd been getting travel brochures for Spain from Canterbury Travel. Maybe that's where he ran off to."

"What's Canterbury Travel?"

"A travel agency here in the village." Harriet had never been inside, but she'd seen the sign in one of the shops in the upper part of town.

"Let's go."

"What? Go?"

"Why not? We can go to the charity shop to ask about the coat, and then to the travel agency to find out if he booked a trip."

"Shouldn't we alert the police to the possibility instead?"

Gemma smiled. "I'm sure they've thought of it already. They're paid to think of things like that. We wouldn't be interfering."

Harriet felt silly. Just because her mind hadn't jumped to the worst option didn't mean the police hadn't thought of it themselves.

"Besides, they may not have discovered who it was he pushed off the cliff—*if* that's what happened—or where he ran to. We could help them." Gemma looked at her eagerly.

Even though Harriet realized how unlikely it all was, it was hard not to get caught up in Gemma's enthusiasm. It would be nice to do something to help figure out what happened. The sooner they found the baron, the sooner he and Coleridge could be reunited. Or the sooner Coleridge could be rehomed, depending on what they found. He was a sweet dog. Maybe she could take him in herself.

But there were some flaws in Gemma's logic. "Are you thinking he pushed someone off a cliff then went to the travel agency and booked a holiday? Wouldn't he get in the car and drive to anywhere but here?"

"He would have left the country, though, right? He couldn't simply drive to Spain or wherever he went."

"I suppose," Harriet said. "But he could have booked a flight on a computer or a phone. Why go to a travel agent for a last-minute flight?"

"How old is he?"

She wasn't sure exactly, but if his younger brother Peter had been friends with Aunt Jinny, and Liam had been married in 1985, she had a guess. "Mid- to late sixties, I would think."

"Some people that age book travel on their phones, but my gran can barely turn hers on. Plus, he's a baron, so he's probably used to having other people do things for him."

Harriet knew plenty of older people who were quite adept with technology, but not all of them were. The baron's laptop was with the police, who were trying to get inside or had by now, so they should be able to tell if he'd booked a flight. But—

"He didn't have a cell phone at all. I forgot about that. So he couldn't have booked a flight that way."

"Well, there you go. If there's a possibility he arranged a flight with a travel agent right here in the village, it can't hurt to ask, can it?"

It likely wouldn't do much good, but Harriet couldn't see how it would hurt either.

"Come on," Gemma said, after draining the last of her tea. "This will be fun. And maybe we'll help solve this thing."

Once again, her new friend's enthusiasm was contagious. Harriet didn't think there was much chance they would dig up anything the police hadn't already, but Gemma made it seem almost irresistible. And maybe they *could* help the police solve the crime.

"All right," Harriet said, finishing her latte. "Let's go."

CHAPTER ELEVEN

Harriet and Gemma started at the charity shop, which Harriet would have called a thrift store. Harriet had noticed the little shop as she'd wandered through the village, but she had never gone inside.

The donation bin stood out front. Most thrift stores Harriet had visited in the States had harsh overhead fluorescents and bare-bones wire-rack shelving, but this shop had warm lighting, wooden shelves, and clothing racks. It felt like a place Harriet would want to browse.

Gemma must have felt the same way, because she headed for the clothing racks rather than the counter to ask about the coat. "Look at this." She held up a loose, flowy dress in a vibrant flower print. "This would be awesome for lounging around the house, wouldn't it?"

Harriet smiled. "Probably, for the right person. How about this?" She grabbed a pink cowboy hat from the top of the rack and put it on. "Makes me feel right at home."

Gemma laughed. "If the accent didn't give it away, that would do it."

Harriet put the cowboy hat back, and they strolled through the home decor. "My granny had something like this in her kitchen," Gemma said, holding up a mauve-and-pink floral valance.

Harriet reached the rack of formal gowns. "This one bears an unfortunate resemblance to my senior prom dress," she said, holding up a pink satin gown with a halter neck and full skirt.

"You must have been the belle of 2009." Gemma laughed. "Mine was a lot shorter, and skintight. My mum nearly lost her mind."

Harriet realized she hadn't laughed so hard in quite a while. She'd suspected Gemma would be fun to hang out with, but she hadn't realized how quickly they'd fall into this kind of friendly banter. They put the dresses back and moved on to the vintage T-shirts.

"This one's actually cool," Gemma said, pulling out a fitted green T-shirt that had two crossed tennis rackets and said ALL ENGLAND LAWN TENNIS AND CROQUET CLUB in a retro font. "That's the private club where Wimbledon is held." She held it up to see if it would fit and then checked the price. Five quid. Done."

She tucked the shirt under her arm and headed for the checkout counter, where a woman about ten years older than Harriet watched them with something like amusement.

"Did you find what you needed?" she asked.

"And more," Gemma said, smiling. "This shop is great."

"We get some really good stuff," the woman said as she rang up the shirt.

"Where do you get your merchandise?" Harriet asked. "Is it mostly donations in the box out front?"

"Mostly, along with things that come in from the churches and a few other organizations in the area."

"Well, we got lucky this time," Gemma said. "You know, I heard about this place because of a jacket someone got in here recently. What was it like again, Harriet?"

"It was black-and-gray houndstooth," Harriet said.

"Ah, yes. I know the one. It was a nice coat—or had been once. It was brought in recently and sold very quickly."

"Did that come in through the donations box?" Gemma asked as she paid for her shirt.

"No, in that case, the person donating the clothing had a whole load, so she brought it all into the shop. I wasn't here at the time, but the owner, Nicola, said it was quite a nice lot."

"Do you know who ended up buying the jacket?" Harriet asked.

"It was a teenager. A bunch of them came in being goofy but ended up buying a number of things, including that coat. I thought it was quite odd for a high school kid to want a coat like that, but I guess these things go in cycles, don't they? What's outdated to one generation is cool and ironic and fun to the next." The woman folded the shirt neatly. "Would you like a bag?"

"No, thank you. It'll fit in mine." Gemma accepted the shirt and slid it into her bag. "Was there anything memorable about the kid who bought it?"

"Not really," the woman said. "I actually think it was Gerald O'Connor's son, but I haven't seen him in years, so it's hard to say."

Harriet had no idea who Gerald O'Connor was, let alone his relatives, but she nodded politely. "Do you remember when you sold the jacket?"

"Must have been last week sometime," she said. "I can't remember the exact day, but I'm pretty sure that's right."

Harriet and Gemma thanked her then stepped back outside.

"So, there you go," Gemma said. "The missing baron's jacket was no longer his. It belonged to some teenage kid. Now we need to figure out why the missing lord wanted to off a teenager."

"Gerald O'Connor's son must have done something bad," Harriet deadpanned.

Gemma laughed. "Okay, fine. That's probably not what happened. Unless the baron had a vendetta against Gerald O'Connor's son for some reason."

"It would make a better story," Harriet said. "But I think the more likely scenario is that some teenagers were down on the beach and one of them left his new jacket behind." She'd seen teens there in the evenings at low tide. Sometimes they lit bonfires.

"You're probably right. But we'd better talk to the travel agent anyway. If the suitcase is missing, Lord Beresford must have gone somewhere, whether he killed someone first or not."

Harriet was starting to think Gemma was having too much fun with the murder theory. If someone had actually died, it wasn't a joking matter.

"Let's hope that's not what happened," she said.

"Of course, but we still should go in and see if the travel agent can tell us whether Lord Beresford recently booked a trip. At least then we can cross that off the list of possibilities."

Harriet had some reservations about the plan, but Gemma seemed so into it, and she didn't want to ruin her friend's fun, not when things were going so well.

"And who knows? Maybe I'll get an idea for my next holiday while we're at it," Gemma said breezily.

Ignoring her misgivings, Harriet led the way to the agency. Canterbury Travel was written in blue on the sign out front, over big plate glass windows displaying photos of white sand beaches with turquoise waters and ones of steep alpine slopes.

"A trip suddenly sounds amazing," Gemma said, admiring the photos. "This won't be hard."

Inside, a low counter separated a small waiting area from a back area with two desks, one of which was occupied.

A woman with graying brown hair peered around her computer and smiled at them. A nameplate on her desk said Brigitte Lindstrom. "Good afternoon. How can I help you?"

Harriet froze. How could she waltz in and ask whether a missing man had gone off on holiday?

Gemma jumped in. "I'm Gemma Loughty, and this my friend Harriet Bailey. She just moved here and took over her grandfather's veterinarian practice."

Brigitte's face lit up. "You must be Doc Bailey's granddaughter. How nice to meet you." She came around the desk to shake hands. "I'm Brigitte. Your grandfather was a wonderful man."

"Thank you for saying so." Harriet smiled. "He was wonderful. I miss him, but I'm grateful to be here."

"We've got something of a strange question," Gemma said. "We're trying to figure out if Lord Beresford might have gone on holiday recently. We were hoping you could tell us whether he'd actually booked a trip."

A shadow crossed Brigitte's face. "Why do you want to know that?"

"I'm taking care of his dog," Harriet said. "It seems he left suddenly, and there was no one to care for his dog, so I've got him. He's sweet, but I'm wondering how long I'll have him. We're trying to figure out when Lord Beresford might be coming back. I don't have any contact information for him. His housekeeper mentioned he'd received several brochures about Spain from this office and that one of his suitcases was missing, so we thought he might have taken a trip after all."

"I see." Brigitte crossed her arms over her chest. "Well, I can tell you what I told the police when they came through here asking the same question an hour ago. Lord Beresford called a few months back and asked for information about booking a holiday to a beach in Spain. I sent him some brochures and followed up several times, but he never responded. If he booked a trip, he didn't do it through this office."

"Do you know why he was suddenly interested in going to Spain?" Gemma asked.

"He didn't mention a reason," Brigitte said. "And I didn't ask."

"Was he planning to go by himself?" Gemma asked.

Harriet thought it was a bold question, but Brigitte answered it. "I don't know that he was truly planning anything, since he never followed through. But I can tell you that when we spoke, he was interested in hearing about hotels with two rooms available. That eliminated some smaller inns and such in popular areas of Costa Brava, so I told him to act quickly before the other hotels were booked, but he never got back to me."

Two rooms for a man who was, by all accounts, a recluse. Who would have been close enough with him to go on vacation together? Daisy?

"And he didn't book anything last-minute recently?" Harriet asked.

"Not through this office," Brigitte repeated. "I do hope everything is all right. It's odd, isn't it, for a man like that to vanish into thin air?"

"We hope everything's all right too," Harriet said. "His dog misses him."

"Let's hope he turns up soon," Gemma said. "Since we're here, I was recently talking with a friend about her favorite Greek island." She pointed to a poster of stark white buildings capped with blue domes and turquoise water below. "If I was interested in booking a holiday to Greece, which islands would you recommend?"

Brigitte lit up. She gestured for them to sit down and launched into a discussion about Santorini vs. Corfu vs. Mykonos. Gemma listened intently, and for a moment, Harriet let herself dream about a trip to sugar-white sands and warm turquoise waters. She and Dustin had briefly floated Greece as a honeymoon destination. Would she want to go without him? She wasn't sure she was ready to face that yet. Fortunately, it was a moot point. Such a trip wasn't possible for her right now, so when Gemma thanked Brigitte and stood to go, several brochures in hand, Harriet was ready.

"Well, that was interesting," Gemma said as soon as they were outside. "Who was Lord Beresford planning to travel with?"

"I don't know, but I sure wish I did," Harriet said. "At least we know he didn't end up booking a trip at all through the agency."

"So where *did* he go?" Gemma said. "We know he didn't fall off the cliff—or at least, the evidence tying him to that spot doesn't check out, so it seems a whole lot less likely. He probably didn't run off to Spain, since I still think he would have scheduled that through the agency. But he must have gone somewhere."

"He could have gone to Spain, if he decided to book a trip on his own," Harriet said. "But I have to believe he would have found accommodation for Coleridge, if it was a trip he'd planned."

"And he probably would have told his housekeeper, including details of where he was going, how long he'd be gone, and how she could reach him," Gemma said. "So we're back to the idea that he left at the last minute. Either because he killed someone and needed to run away before the body was discovered—"

"Which seems unlikely," Harriet said. She really wished Gemma would stop harping on that theory.

"Which could be true, but let's hope it's not," Gemma said with clear reluctance. "Or he had another reason to suddenly skip town without telling anyone, even his housekeeper. He had to know she would worry about him."

"Whatever the reason is, hopefully it explains why there were signs of a struggle in his study and why someone has been lurking around my place since Coleridge came to stay."

Gemma's eyes widened. "Harriet, it's not safe for you to be there if some creep is sneaking around your property."

"He's run away both times I've seen him," Harriet said. "I get the sense he's interested in the dog, not me."

"It doesn't matter. It's not safe."

Harriet considered it, but she felt plenty safe, especially with Coleridge around.

"Well, hopefully the police figure out what happened to Lord Beresford quickly. I think we're stuck." Gemma checked her watch. "I should get going, but if you learn anything, you have to let me know."

Harriet promised she would, and the two said their goodbyes. She headed back up to the Land Rover and drove to Polly's to pick up Coleridge then headed home. There was still a car in front of the gallery, but Aunt Jinny didn't seem to be home. She took Coleridge off the leash inside the house, and he meandered around, sniffing.

Gazing around, Harriet thought she should probably do some cleaning. There were always a hundred things to do with a house this size. She could do the laundry or make dinner. But the events of the day kept playing through her mind, and she couldn't stop thinking about the missing baron and the things she'd learned.

She was glad the coat hadn't been in Lord Beresford's possession when it ended up on the beach. However, it didn't eliminate the possibility that he'd fallen when the cliff crumbled, nor did it explain why Coleridge had been so interested in that spot.

But bloodhounds had extremely sensitive noses and could pick up scents at great distances. It was possible that he'd pulled Harriet to that spot on the cliff because he smelled the coat below, and with it the scent of his master. Even with the newer smells that would have been on the coat—like the scent of its new owner and seawater—she didn't think it was out of the realm of possibility that the scent of the coat was what had led Coleridge to that spot.

Either way, it seemed safe to cross off the theory that he'd fallen to his death, for which Harriet was very glad.

And as much as Gemma had liked the idea, Harriet didn't think it was particularly likely that Lord Beresford had killed someone and fled before his crime was discovered. Aunt Jinny had said that he was unpleasant, but that didn't mean he was capable of murder. It was possible, she supposed, if he had a reason—to protect someone he loved, for instance—or if he'd snapped, but it didn't seem likely. Besides, there were no reports of anyone else missing from the area. Harriet felt that Gemma had probably listened to too many true-crime podcasts, and the murder theory was probably not worth spending any more time on.

The mail from End Peerage Now was interesting. Did someone from that group have something to do with this? She made a mental note to dig into that.

And then there was the matter of the missing suitcase. The most likely scenario was that the baron had gone somewhere quite suddenly, given the fact that he'd left Coleridge uncared for and Mrs. Lewis didn't know about the trip. But where had he gone? The fact that he hadn't booked a trip through the travel agency didn't mean he hadn't gone at all. He could have booked a trip on his computer, or simply gone to the airport or train station and bought a ticket. But according to Brigitte, he'd been planning on booking two rooms, which implied that he'd meant to take someone with him, at least at one time.

Who was Daisy to him, really? Was she the one he'd intended to go on holiday with? By all accounts, a trip was out of character for him, but wasn't love a likely reason for someone to do something wildly out of character? Was it love, or were they good friends? Did Daisy know where Lord Beresford had gone?

Or had he intended to go with one of his sons? Did either of them know where he was? She imagined the police had been in contact with both sons and wondered what they had said, whether they knew where their father had gone.

She sat down at the table, opened her laptop, and pulled up the social media profiles of his two children once more. Neither Edward nor Stuart had posted anything about their father's disappearance. That wasn't unusual, given the highly curated nature of their feeds. The news of a missing baron was not flattering, and they seemed to only post pictures that showed them and their families in a complimentary light.

Then again, didn't everyone? Harriet hadn't been on social media much since her breakup, but before that she'd posted plenty of pictures of herself and Dustin in beautiful settings—cute cafés, rolling hills, even on the beach showing off the engagement ring right after he proposed. She usually tried to keep bad news off her feed. She hadn't even announced the end of the relationship. She'd simply gone off social media altogether. So the fact that his sons hadn't posted anything about their father's disappearance wasn't too surprising.

There was also the possibility that they knew exactly where he was and there was nothing strange going on at all. But how could she find out?

If Edward or Stuart knew something, they would have told DC Worthington or DI McCormick, who were unlikely to pass on any information to a nosy local vet. But Harriet was caring for the baron's dog unexpectedly, and she didn't know when or if the baron was coming home. It wouldn't be that strange for her to reach out and ask if they had any idea where he'd gone and when he would be back. She wasn't some random lookie-loo, drawn by the sordid news. She was trying to find out how long she'd be looking after Coleridge.

It wasn't hard to find email addresses online for both Edward and Stuart. Edward's email address was on the webpage of a charity he championed, and she located Stuart's through the Contact button on his woodworking website. She worded the emails carefully, introducing herself as the veterinarian in White Church Bay and explaining that she was boarding their father's dog. She asked if they knew when he might return then hit Send before she could talk herself out of it.

Another theory involved the group End Peerage Now. Harriet had poked around on their website, but now that she'd seen the letters they'd sent to the baron, they seemed like less of a distant possibility and more of a real threat.

She returned to the website for the group and clicked through the pages again. The page of mailing addresses for the gentry bothered her. Were these people all getting letters like Lord Beresford's? Why did the group think sending them would get them closer to their goal? If these families had held on to their titles and land for hundreds of years, they weren't likely to give them up because of a threatening piece of mail.

She found the message board again and started to read through the entries. There were a lot of posts about how to get to London and cheap places to stay in the city for various protests the group was organizing. Harriet didn't mind that, but it didn't seem relevant for what she needed.

Mrs. Lewis had said that the letters for the baron had started arriving around five years ago. She scrolled back through the messages until she came to posts from that time. She scanned the headlines there.

ORGANIZING A PROTEST—BEST MEGAPHONE AND WHERE TO GET IT CHEAPLY?
GETTING A MESSAGE TO HE WHO MUST NOT BE NAMED, AKA LEADER OF THE HOUSE?

Updated List of Titleholders (aka Who's Died Recently)
Vacation Pics of Shadow Leader of the House—Check Out That Boat!

Charming. Harriet didn't totally disagree with the point that the system was unfair, but she strongly disagreed with their methods.

She clicked through some of the topics and studied the usernames who had posted and commented. Maybe she could figure out the identity of the person the letters had come from, which might lead to discovering whether they had anything to do with Lord Beresford's disappearance. Based on what she was seeing, she had to agree with Mrs. Lewis's sentiment that she hoped whatever had happened to him didn't involve this group.

The letter she'd seen today had been mailed from Leeds, so she was looking for someone from that part of the country, and ideally someone who had posted something about mailing letters around that time, or someone who had joined the group around then.

There was someone who posted as HouseMouse. She clicked on the link below the name and was taken to a profile page. HouseMouse was listed as twenty-nine, female, and living in Brighton. Her profile picture was of a gray wig, like the one worn by the members of the House of Lords, with a red *X* through it. Who knew whether any of her personal information was true, but assuming it was, Harriet wasn't looking for someone from Brighton, and this user had been active for two years before the time frame she wanted.

Another user called himself UncleSonny. He didn't post much on his own but responded to a lot of questions. His profile claimed he was fifty-two and lived in Sheffield. His profile picture was of an orange cat. He'd been silent on the forum for nearly three years, which she thought made him unlikely to be the person still sending letters to Lord Beresford.

Another user posted a few questions about the mailing addresses on the site. Harriet selected the username UnitedForever and found a profile picture of a yellow-and-blue logo shaped like a shield. UnitedForever had joined the site and started posting almost exactly five years before, which was about the time the letters had started arriving at Beresford Manor. UnitedForever was listed as male, thirty-three—and living in Leeds.

That was interesting. Who was this UnitedForever? She read through the posts he'd made or commented on. Most of his posts had to do with letters, which he appeared to be mailing to the names listed on the site in Yorkshire. This had to be him. But who was he? She kept reading and found that he referenced a career in IT in one post, and a flat—apartment—near a fire station in another. There was a post about a football game and another about the price of stamps. This wasn't getting her anywhere.

What about that logo? She focused on the profile picture. The shield had a flower of some kind at the top, and yellow-and-blue diagonal stripes below, with the letters *LUFC* running down the middle. What was that?

She tried a reverse image search in a new browser tab and found that it was the logo of the Leeds United Football Club. Apparently, it was the logo of the local soccer team in the Premier League. UnitedForever must be a reference to that. Whoever this guy was, he was a big fan. But plenty of people in the UK were fans of one football team or another.

She went back to the post about the football game. He'd included a selfie of himself cheering. He'd pasted a soccer ball sticker over his face, so that wasn't helpful.

On a whim, she plugged the photo into the reverse image search page. There it was. The search engine displayed the same photo, but this time it didn't have the soccer ball over his face.

She'd found the man who had been harassing Lord Beresford for years.

CHAPTER TWELVE

The man appeared to be in his early thirties, as his profile said, and he had short dishwater-blond hair and pale skin. In the football photo, he wore a shirt with the Leeds United logo on it. She clicked on the picture and found that it was also being used as a profile picture on a social media page for a man named Leon Evans. Leon was an IT manager for a medical device company in Leeds and posted several pictures of himself with his cat, Sir Cuddles.

The page made Leon appear considerably less frightening than he'd sounded in the letter about the coming revolution. Still, the letter was alarming, and if Leon was behind it, then she should probably alert the police.

She pulled out her phone and dialed the number for DC Worthington.

"Hello?" She heard low sounds and voices in the background, which meant he was probably out in public somewhere.

"Hello, Van. It's Harriet Bailey."

"Hi, Harriet. What's going on?"

"Is there any news on Lord Beresford?" Maybe they'd located him and all of this was pointless anyway.

"We're working on it," Van said in a weary tone that told her he'd answered that exact question the same way many times recently. "We're following up on all leads."

That meant no. In that case, she would tell him what she'd learned.

"I had to go pick up some medicine for his dog today, so I went by Beresford Manor. While I was there, Mrs. Lewis told me about some letters that were sent by a member of a group called End Peerage Now."

"Yes, she showed me the letters when we went by the house. We bagged them and are testing for fingerprints."

Harriet took a deep breath. "The thing is, I was poking around on the group's website, and I think I may have figured out who sent them."

"You what?"

"His name is Leon Evans, and he's an IT manager in Leeds." Van was quiet, and in her nervousness, she rushed to fill the silence. "He has a cat."

"Hang on. I'm writing this down," he said. "Now, how did you figure this out?"

She recounted her thought process and the research she'd done, and Van let out a low whistle.

"That's a lot of digging," he said.

"Yes, well, I'm concerned," she said. "Coleridge wants his master back."

"Speaking of the dog, we're trying to find the man who's been hanging around your clinic, but we haven't had much luck. We were hoping to get CCTV footage from the road that would show his license plate, but there aren't many cameras out your way."

Harriet was glad of that in general, though she wished for some at the current moment.

"We'll check out this Leon bloke, and I'll let you know if we find anything on the license plate or the lurker," Van said. "Did you see the article in the paper this morning?"

"I did," Harriet confirmed.

"That story didn't come from us. We want to be careful about what gets out there, so please don't talk to the press."

Anxiety washed over her. She'd just spent all afternoon with a member of the press.

But Gemma had said she hadn't written the story, and Harriet had told Gemma that everything they discussed at lunch was off the record. That meant Gemma couldn't print anything they'd talked about. She was safe. Right? Still, she probably shouldn't tell Gemma so much in the future.

"Harriet?"

"I won't talk to the press," she assured him.

When they hung up, she felt unsettled. She decided to send a text to Gemma. The last thing she wanted was to be responsible for messing up the police investigation into the missing baron.

JUST CONFIRMING. EVERYTHING WE TALKED ABOUT TODAY IS OFF THE RECORD, RIGHT?

OF COURSE! Gemma texted back right away. SO FUN HANGING OUT WITH YOU TODAY. HAVE A GREAT NIGHT, FRIEND!

That confirmed it. She hadn't messed up anything. It wouldn't be printed. And she'd given the police a new lead. She still wasn't sure whether it would get them any closer to finding the baron. If End Peerage Now was involved somehow, the most likely scenario for his disappearance probably involved kidnapping. She shuddered at the thought. The rumpled rug, overturned table, and broken glass seemed to point toward that possibility, but the missing suitcase indicated instead that he'd gone away of his own free will.

Her stomach growled, and she pushed herself to her feet. It was past time for dinner. She rooted around in the fridge and pulled out some cheese and a few pieces of bread, reminding herself that she needed to go to the grocery store. She made herself a grilled cheese sandwich—or a cheese toastie, the local term that she preferred, although a toaster wasn't involved. After she finished the sandwich and a cup of yogurt, she stood up and stretched. Charlie meowed, rubbing against Harriet's legs, which was how she signaled that her food bowl was empty. Harriet fed the dogs and cat then gave Coleridge the medicine she'd taken from the clinic. He took it easily, which confirmed to her that he was used to the routine.

"Ready to go for a walk, Coleridge?" The dog hopped to his feet and wagged his tail, making her chuckle. "You like that word, don't you?" She clipped on his leash. She grabbed a sweater and her phone, thinking she would try to call Sylvia while she walked. But when she got outside, she saw that Aunt Jinny was sitting across the grounds at the table in her garden, drinking a cup of tea. A small plate of biscuits, which Harriet would have called cookies, was on the table.

"Hi, Aunt Jinny," she called, swerving in that direction.

"Hello, Harriet." Aunt Jinny smiled at her. "Nice night, isn't it?"

It was. The sun had broken through the clouds, and the evening air cast everything in a soft golden glow.

Aunt Jinny gestured to the chair across from her. "Would you like to sit? I'll even share my favorite shortbread. I don't share them with just anyone, so you should feel special."

"I do feel special, but I was about to take Coleridge for a walk, and I probably shouldn't let him down." It would be nice to talk to Aunt Jinny though. Maybe she could help Harriet process all that had happened today. "Any chance I could talk you into coming along?"

"A walk does sound nice." Aunt Jinny finished her piece of shortbread, set her teacup in its saucer, and pushed herself up. "It might help me clear my head. I'll clean this up when I get back."

The women fell into step, and Coleridge walked along quietly in front of them, his nose to the ground.

"Rough day?" Aunt Jinny asked.

"Certainly a confusing one."

"I suppose that's to be expected, since you're still settling in," Aunt Jinny said.

"I guess so." They walked beside the low rock wall along the front edge of the property, heading toward the cliffs. Harriet could hear the pounding waves below.

"Have you heard anything more about the missing baron?" Aunt Jinny asked.

Harriet threw up her free hand in frustration. "I've heard he's either been kidnapped by an anti-peerage fringe group, or run away on holiday without telling anyone, or he's killed someone and is in hiding."

"Goodness."

"I'm not sure which of those is true. Likely none of them."

"I heard that the houndstooth jacket has been linked to a teenager and they no longer think Liam fell off the cliff and drowned," Aunt Jinny said. "So that's good news."

"Yes, the coat was donated to a charity shop. The working theory is that some kid bought it and left it on the beach."

"Probably at a get-together down there. That happens a lot in the summer at low tide."

"That sounds likely." Harriet waited while Coleridge sniffed at a particularly interesting patch of grass. "Do you know anything about Daisy Lyons?"

"Sure. Well, I know of her. She's from an old family around these parts. She's maybe ten years older than me. She's always been a patron of the arts and owns several of your grandfather's paintings." Aunt Jinny pulled her cardigan closer as the breeze kicked up. "She breeds and shows dogs, I believe."

"Coleridge is one of hers. Apparently, she gave him to Lord Beresford."

"That makes sense."

"I heard that she and the baron might be more than friends, but nobody seems to know for sure."

"You hear all kinds of rumors, but I suppose you never really know. Not that it's anyone's business but theirs."

That was a thoroughly unsatisfying answer. Harriet tried again. "I gather Polly thinks they were in love once but they weren't allowed to marry. But she also said Daisy is distantly related to the royal family, so I don't understand why not. Wouldn't anyone want to marry into the royal family?"

"I couldn't say if they were in love," Aunt Jinny said. "That's between them, I suppose. But I can say that being related to royals is not necessarily all it's cracked up to be."

"But isn't that the goal of this whole peerage thing? To have as high a rank as possible? And it doesn't get any higher than the royal family, does it? Why wouldn't they be allowed to marry?" Even as she said the words, she realized the obvious answer. "Oh. *He* wasn't good enough for *her*, was he? A mere baron?"

"It sounds like you've learned about this system by reading too many novels." Aunt Jinny laughed. "There are plenty of reasons people don't marry—even people in the nobility. I don't know for sure whether or not it's true they weren't allowed to marry or why. But I can tell you that it costs far more than you'd think to keep an estate going. It used to be that the lord of the manor was the land-lord for everyone around him, and everyone worked for him. He got a significant income from his lands. It's not like that anymore, and inheriting a title and house doesn't necessarily come with the money to keep it up."

"The baron doesn't get paid to be the lord of Beresford Manor?"

"I'm sure the family has money stashed away earning interest," Aunt Jinny said. "And I imagine he rents out the farmland owned by the estate. But they've sold off the workers' cottages and much of the land, so I imagine it's still not enough. That's why you see so many of these old houses coming up for sale."

"You're saying maybe money was the reason they didn't marry." They came to the edge of the property, where the driveway met up with the road, and beyond that, the path that ran along the cliffs. Harriet breathed deeply, inhaling the smell of the salty air.

"I'm speculating," Aunt Jinny said. "Daisy comes from an old family, but they ended up selling off most of their land and several of the buildings some years back. And I'm pointing out that Liam's late wife's family didn't come from the gentry, but her father was a wealthy businessman."

"So Liam couldn't marry Daisy because he had to marry someone rich to maintain the family estate?"

"That's what you hear. But like I said, you never really know what's going on in someone else's life."

Harriet supposed it was true. From the outside, she and Dustin had seemed like the perfect couple, even while their relationship was slowly falling apart.

"Why the curiosity about Daisy?" Aunt Jinny asked.

"I'm supposed to meet with her tomorrow," Harriet said. "I sent her an email because I hoped she could give me proof that Coleridge is a purebred bloodhound."

"If he's one of hers, he surely is."

"I know, but the police need hard evidence to give credence to the idea that someone might be trying to dognap Coleridge."

"Do you think the man we saw could possibly be related to Daisy in some way?" Aunt Jinny asked.

"I hadn't thought of that," Harriet said, startled by the idea. "It would explain how Coleridge knows him, if he was around when Coleridge was a puppy. Dogs have better memories than people give them credit for, especially when they're tied to scent."

"You might want to ask her about him when you see her," Aunt Jinny said.

They walked in silence for a few moments. Harriet mulled over the conversation, and her mind played back something Aunt Jinny had said.

"How did you know that the coat belonged to a kid on the beach instead of the baron?" she asked.

"Van let me know when he and DI McCormick came into my clinic this afternoon," Aunt Jinny said. "They were asking questions about Lord Beresford."

"At your office?" Harriet peered at her aunt, trying to read her impassive face.

Aunt Jinny didn't answer for a moment, but then she said, "They wanted to know his blood type."

"Why would they want that?"

"There was blood on the broken glass of the decanter that was found in his study, wasn't there?" Aunt Jinny reminded her.

"That's right," Harriet said. It was one of the more haunting details from the scene in the study.

"First, they asked me about DNA, but I don't keep DNA from my patients. I do keep the results of blood tests though. I suppose they're testing the blood. If it's not Liam's blood type, then they know it came from someone else."

"Will they be able to figure out whose it is?"

"I don't know. They did ask about the blood types of every member of the family, so I suppose they're casting their net wide."

"And you were able to give them that information?" Weren't there privacy laws in the UK, like there were in the US? Doctors back home couldn't go around handing out people's medical information to whoever asked, even if it was a police officer.

"They had a warrant for the information," Aunt Jinny said. "I'm not sure what evidence they provided the judge to convince her they needed that information, but I had to comply. I suppose it means they've stepped up the search and are very serious about finding the baron."

"I guess so." Harriet thought for a moment. "So was the blood his?"

"I don't know. I have no idea what type of blood they found on the glass."

"I guess it's a good thing they're following that lead," Harriet said. "And hopefully it will lead them to him, wherever he is."

"Let's hope so."

They fell into a companionable silence again, each lost in her own thoughts. The waves crashed on the beach below, and the breeze carried the softest hints of clover and honeysuckle.

"I heard you hung out with that reporter again today," Aunt Jinny said.

"My goodness. The gossip network in this town truly is something."

Aunt Jinny smiled. "It's a small town."

"Who told you?"

"Pauline at the charity shop is a friend."

"What did she say?"

"That you were there and had a good time with the reporter. And that you'd asked about the coat."

"She's the one who told us it was sold to a teenager."

Aunt Jinny nodded. "Be careful with her."

"With Pauline?"

"No, dear. With the reporter."

"But she's great. We have so much in common, and she's really fun."

"I'm not sure I trust her."

Heat rose in Harriet's cheeks. "You don't know her. That's not fair."

"I know. I'm merely encouraging you to think about what she wants."

"The same as I want. Someone her own age to hang out with."

Aunt Jinny took in a long breath and let it out slowly. "Perhaps."

"What do you mean? What else would she want?"

"The British press isn't like it is in the States," Aunt Jinny said. "They're more aggressive. More invasive. They'll stop at nothing to get a story."

"That's not what this was about," Harriet protested. "She's a junior reporter. She's writing a puff piece about me taking over Grandad's practice."

Though now that she thought about it, Gemma had said she wanted to get together so she could ask some follow-up questions about the piece, but she never had. She'd started in on the missing lord almost immediately.

"Did she ask you about the baron while she was at it?"

"Yes," Harriet said. "We did talk about it some. But I told her everything was off the record, so she can't print any of it."

Aunt Jinny hesitated, as if formulating her response. "Just be careful, okay? That's all I'm saying."

"I will." Harriet didn't understand. She and Gemma had had so much fun together. It was unusual to find someone like that, someone she clicked with so easily. It was so hard to move to a new place and not know anyone.

"Has Claire reached out to you yet?" Aunt Jinny asked.

"Yes. I ran into her in the village, and she invited me over for a barbecue on Friday evening."

"That's nice. I think you'll like her."

Harriet was dubious, but she knew better than to say so. It was worth investing one evening in possibly making a friend. "I'm looking forward to it," she said, mainly because she knew it was what Aunt Jinny wanted to hear.

Shortly after that, they headed home. They said goodbye on Harriet's doorstep, and Harriet took Maxwell out one last time. She thought about calling one of her friends back home, but it was getting late, and she was wiped out. The time difference really made it hard. She'd call another time.

She climbed into bed. As she tried to fall asleep, her mind kept going over her visit with Gemma. Aunt Jinny was totally off base. Harriet was sure of it. She hadn't laughed like that since she'd moved here. She was finally making a real friend. Why did Aunt Jinny want to ruin that, after it had been her idea for Harriet to make more of an effort in her social life in the first place? Did she want to pick Harriet's friends now?

But at the edge of Harriet's mind, doubts crept in, no matter how hard she tried to push them away. First of all, she knew her aunt wasn't like that. And why hadn't Gemma ever asked the follow-up questions about the interview? That was what she'd wanted to talk about, wasn't it?

Maybe it was an innocent pretense for getting together. Gemma had realized they could be friends too, and instead of suggesting they get together and hang out, she'd used the piece as an excuse. Surely there wasn't any more to it than that.

But another question slid into her mind. Gemma had said Harriet must have been the belle of the ball in her 2009 prom dress. Harriet *had* gone to her senior prom in 2009, but how had Gemma known that? Harriet hadn't told her exactly how old she was. Was she assuming they were roughly the same age and guessing at a year? It was a strangely specific year to guess.

Then again, it wasn't that bizarre. Gemma was a reporter, after all. She'd probably done some basic research on Harriet to flesh out the piece about the vet practice. It wouldn't have been hard to find out what year Harriet had graduated from high school.

Everything was aboveboard. There was nothing to worry about.

And yet somehow, she couldn't stop doing just that.

CHAPTER THIRTEEN

Harriet woke to bright sunshine. From her high, antique bed, she had a wonderful view out over the gardens and toward the rolling farmland beyond. She took a minute to lie in bed and thank the Lord for this amazing place, for bringing her here, and for all the blessings of this new life. She prayed for her parents and her friends in the States, for Aunt Jinny, and for Liam Beresford, wherever he was. She prayed that he would be found soon, safe and sound.

Eventually, she climbed out of bed and made her way downstairs. Coleridge and Maxwell greeted her at the bottom of the stairs, but Charlie barely acknowledged her from a perch on the back of the couch.

Harriet didn't have any appointments scheduled for first thing that morning, but she checked her phone anyway. Sometimes she had messages from frantic farmers who'd woken to discover a sick animal, but that wasn't the case this morning. She had nothing until the farm visit out near Daisy's home in a couple of hours.

She made a cup of coffee, hooked up Maxwell's wheels, and took both dogs out, scanning for the strange man to make sure Coleridge was safe. She didn't see anything out of the ordinary. The sky was a brilliant robin's-egg blue, and the sweet smell of the roses and honeysuckle combined with the smell of salty air. Maxwell bounced around in front of Coleridge, trying to get the big dog to chase him, but Coleridge mostly ignored him and sniffed the garden intently. After a few minutes Harriet took them in and fed them, taking a moment to be grateful that Coleridge was back on his medication.

Charlie wound between her legs and mewed.

"I didn't forget you," she said, opening a can of cat food. Charlie started eating, and suddenly the house was quiet.

Harriet nursed her cup of coffee while she read her Bible and made herself a quick breakfast of eggs, fresh from a nearby farm, and toast.

After breakfast, she scanned her email. She had one from Stuart Beresford, Lord Beresford's second son. She opened it eagerly.

> *Dr. Bailey,*
>
> *Thank you for your message. The police have also been in touch, and I wish I had a better answer for you. I don't know where my father has gone, and my brother doesn't know either. I will say I'm quite surprised that he would have left without making proper arrangements for Coleridge. He loves that dog more than anything. If you hear from him, please let him know that his sons would appreciate being notified before he goes on any other journeys, as these inquiries have become quite disruptive.*
>
> *Sincerely,*
> *Stuart Beresford*

Harriet had to read the email twice to make sure she understood it correctly. Was he—did he see his father's mysterious disappearance as an inconvenience? Was he really so callous? She reminded herself that it was hard to convey tone in an email, and that the British were famous for their reserve, so she might be reading it wrong. But she couldn't think of any other way to interpret that last line.

She thanked the Lord for her good relationship with her parents. She would have called them to check in, but it was way too early in Connecticut. She'd try to touch base with them later.

She caught up on the rest of her emails before pushing herself up to get ready for the day. She showered and dressed and then let Maxwell and Charlie into the clinic. Polly hadn't arrived yet, but they would be fine until she did. Harriet loaded Coleridge into the old Rover and headed out.

The Hamilton farm was nestled in a little hollow on the back side of a craggy hill, surrounded in all directions by the rolling moors. Woolly sheep dotted the hillsides, and the farm itself was comprised of a neat stone farmhouse, as well as several wooden barns and outbuildings. Harriet left Coleridge inside the vehicle with the windows cracked.

Leslie Hamilton greeted Harriet and led her past a small yarn shop—where she sold wool that she'd carded, spun, and dyed herself—and into the barn, where pens lined the walls, holding dozens of sheep. Many of the animals bleated when the door opened. Harriet smiled at the sound as she followed Leslie to the pens.

Harriet gave the sheep their shots and checked them over to make sure they were in good health before she waved goodbye and set the GPS on her phone to the address Daisy Lyons had given her. It was about a twenty-minute drive, and the route took Harriet through several picturesque villages and across rolling hills. The GPS eventually led her around a small hill and over a rise, and after a long drive down a bumpy driveway, the stately brick home stood flanked by a grove of trees. The Georgian-style home was three stories, with symmetrical wings and triangular pediments over the front door and windows. A light-colored stone outbuilding stood to the side of the main house, alongside a pathway lined with carefully tended rosebushes.

Harriet wished she'd thought to bring clothes to change into as she walked up to the front door, her rubber boots flopping against the gravel drive. Coleridge's tail wagged as he led her eagerly toward the house. Before they reached the door, it opened, and a woman with gray hair tied up under a handkerchief stepped out. She wore dark green slacks and an Irish wool cardigan with Wellington boots, which the British called wellies.

"You must be Harriet," she said with a wide smile. "I can see your grandfather in you, all right."

Coleridge strained at the leash, his tail wagging as he let out a series of excited barks.

"And hello to you, Coleridge," Daisy said, leaning down to pet the dog. "You're quite well, aren't you?" She straightened again. "I thought we might walk over to the kennel and see the puppies if you're interested."

"I would love that," Harriet said. "I never get tired of puppies."

Daisy chuckled and led them on the brick path toward the outbuilding. "I want to know more about you and hear about how you're liking Yorkshire, but please forgive an old woman's curiosity first. What's going on with Liam, and why are you caring for

Coleridge? It wasn't clear in your message, but it sounded like something strange is going on."

"It is," Harriet said. "No one seems to know where Lord Beresford has gone."

"Oh dear. What do you mean, no one seems to know?" The shock on her face appeared genuine, which told Harriet that she didn't know where Liam was. It also told her that the police hadn't been along to talk to Daisy yet, but they could be pursuing more promising leads. This might be a fool's errand after all. Oh, well. At least she would get to see some puppies.

"His suitcase is missing," Harriet said, "But he didn't inform Mrs. Lewis he was going anywhere or leave any message behind. And there were signs of a scuffle in his study—"

"A scuffle?" Daisy repeated, alarmed.

"The rug was pushed up and a table had been overturned. A decanter was smashed."

"That doesn't sound good."

It was such a typically British understatement that Harriet wanted to laugh.

"And then Coleridge was found loose in town, which seemed to suggest Lord Beresford might have left in a hurry, before he had a chance to find boarding for him."

"That's very unlike Liam. There was nothing in his diary?"

"Not according to Mrs. Lewis."

"Perhaps she should check again. If Liam had anything planned, it would have been there. He recorded everything—all his appointments, meetings, notes, everything. If there's truly nothing, that's a very bad sign indeed."

"So you haven't heard from him?" Harriet asked.

"No," Daisy said. The scent of roses and lavender hung in the air as they walked down the brick path. "We're usually in touch every few weeks or so, but I think he would have mentioned something to me about going on holiday, perhaps to see if I could look after Coleridge. He hasn't been on a trip in quite some time. Not since the disastrous trip to Toronto when his grandson was born."

"Disastrous?"

"That's right. He and Stuart have never gotten on well, and since Beatrice passed, it's gotten even worse. Anyway, every time I've tried to convince him to go on a trip with me, he's flat-out refused. I guess that doesn't mean he couldn't have gone, but it doesn't seem like him."

"You've tried to convince him to travel?" Harriet was trying to grasp the nature of their relationship, and not getting many clues. Most couples she knew talked more often than every few weeks, but every relationship was different. And that assumed Daisy was telling the truth about the frequency of their contact.

"I pushed for Spain last year. Julius and I went to Barcelona one summer and saw all the Gaudí architecture. Liam would love it. He's fascinated by that kind of thing. But he wouldn't hear of it."

"Why not?"

"He always says travel is too much."

"Too much?"

"Hassle. Money. Change." She shrugged. "And maybe that's all true. Or maybe he didn't want to go with me. I couldn't say for sure."

"You've been friends a long time, I heard," Harriet said, hoping she would take the bait.

"We grew up together. At one point we even thought we might marry, but our families had other ideas." Harriet was about to apologize, but Daisy waved it away before she spoke. "It was for the best, really. We make good friends, and I think romance would have ruined it." She frowned. "I know there are some who wonder, but I've never thought it worth the energy to disabuse them of the idea. People will think what they think, won't they? Especially if I try to correct them. But Liam and I are close friends, nothing more."

Daisy slid the big wooden barn door aside. Harriet heard the chirps and cries of puppies as they stepped inside.

"Apparently, Lord Beresford was getting brochures from a travel agent, trying to sell him a trip to Spain," Harriet said. "It seems he called the shop and asked about booking a trip."

"Really?" Daisy cocked her head. "Well now. Maybe I got through to him more than I thought. Perhaps he went after all. I wish he'd told me, but if he did go, I'm glad for him. I think it'll do him a world of good."

Harriet dropped Coleridge's leash, and he galloped ahead of her, leading the way down the long row between two sets of pens, toward the yipping puppies.

"Maybe," Harriet said. "A suitcase is gone, but Mrs. Lewis couldn't say if his passport was gone or not, as she didn't know the combination to the safe where he kept it. But the travel agent did say he hadn't booked a trip through her."

"Perhaps he booked it on his own. That would be a happy ending, wouldn't it? A surprise holiday?"

"It would be," Harriet said.

They passed empty stalls that were no doubt meant for horses and sheep. But the large pen at the end of the row held a mother bloodhound and half a dozen puppies. They were adorable, with big floppy ears and squishy faces and huge paws. Two of the pups were unsteady on their feet as they wobbled around the pen. Harriet guessed they were about four weeks old.

"They're adorable," she said.

"Would you like to hold one?"

"Yes please," she answered eagerly.

Daisy opened the pen and scooped up a tiny wriggling dog. Harriet accepted the puppy from her. It squirmed and licked her face, making her laugh.

"This litter is almost five weeks old," Daisy said proudly. "They'll be going to their new homes in about three weeks."

"They're purebred, of course," Harriet said.

"All of mine are."

"Including Coleridge?"

"Sure enough. He's one of my finest."

Harriet had known it was true, but it felt good to have it confirmed.

As she cuddled the puppy, Harriet couldn't help asking, "Are they all spoken for?" The last thing she needed was a puppy, but holding this one, she let herself daydream.

"Yes, they are. I have a waiting list more than a year long," Daisy said. "I could sell a lot more if I scaled up and got more dogs, but I couldn't provide the kind of care these dogs need if I did that, so I never have. It's not about the money for me." She leaned over and stroked Coleridge's head, and he wagged his tail, gazing up at her in open adoration.

It did seem like a well-run operation. Harriet held the squirming puppy against her chest. It was so soft and sweet. "You gave Coleridge to Lord Beresford, right?"

"I did. The next person on the list had to wait until the next litter but didn't mind. Liam needed something to get him out of the house. He was so lonely. At first he was upset and tried to refuse, but even he couldn't resist the charms of a bloodhound puppy." Daisy rubbed Coleridge's head. "He's never admitted I was right, but we both know I was. He loves Coleridge." Coleridge's tail thumped against the side of the pen.

"I've heard that too," Harriet said.

Daisy raised troubled eyes to hers. "That's why I'm so confused by the whole thing. He wouldn't just skip town and leave Coleridge behind without someone to care for him. Does the clinic still offer boarding services?"

"Yes," Harriet said. "We care for our patients however we can."

"I thought so. He knew about that option. And even if your kennels weren't available, he could have brought Coleridge here. I told Liam I would be happy to care for him if Liam ever did take a trip. So it worries me that Coleridge was found wandering around."

Harriet hesitated, not wanting to upset her even more, but decided to ask her next question. "Do you know of anyone who might be trying to dognap Coleridge?"

Daisy started. "What? Is someone after him?"

Harriet told her about the strange man who'd been lurking around her property and that Coleridge had clearly recognized him.

"Purebred dogs are sometimes stolen," Daisy said sadly. "Mostly for resale, since they can be quite valuable. I sure hope that's not the case. You think this strange fellow had something to do with Liam leaving?"

"He only showed up once I had Coleridge at my place, and Coleridge reacted to him. Part of me wonders if he's what the fight in the study was about. Perhaps someone was there to take Coleridge," Harriet mused. "But then how did they end up leaving without him?"

"And why would someone go to all that trouble for a four-year-old dog?" Daisy asked. "As lovely as he is, Coleridge would probably fetch a few hundred pounds at most. A puppy would get much more."

Harriet suspected that some people would consider a few hundred pounds well worth the hassle of stealing a dog, but Daisy was already continuing.

"I would guess a dognapping would typically involve someone sneaking around to take the dog, not confronting the owner inside his home," Daisy said. "I suppose it could have been someone hoping to take Coleridge and hold him for ransom. It's no secret how much Liam loves this dog. But I still can't see how that would lead to the scene you're describing in the study."

"Maybe someone had already dognapped Coleridge and was talking to Liam about the fee to return him? And Lord Beresford got so mad he threw the decanter?"

"But Coleridge is here, not dognapped," Daisy said. "A dognapper wouldn't have let him go until he had his money."

"And that theory doesn't explain where Lord Beresford is now," Harriet said. "Or why he took his suitcase and disappeared."

"True. If it wasn't a dognapper he was talking to in his study, who was it?" Daisy mused.

"Does Lord Beresford have any enemies?"

"I doubt it. There were people who didn't like Liam, I imagine. He wasn't always pleasant to everyone. But just because he didn't always adhere to the niceties doesn't mean someone would want to hurt him." Daisy snapped her fingers. "There's that group who's trying to abolish the peerage. But unless he let one of them into his home to have a conversation, which doesn't seem likely, I can't see how that would work."

"I guess you're right," Harriet said. "The police have the name of the man who sent him threatening letters, but you're right. I doubt the two of them were having a conversation in his study." Now that she thought about it like that, it sounded extremely implausible.

"Liam isn't the most outgoing man, but there aren't too many people who evoke enough emotion to spark a scene like the one you're describing," Daisy said.

"What do you mean?"

"It's not too hard to ignore people you don't like, even if they're being horrible. There's emotional distance, I suppose. But usually it takes someone you care about to make you angry enough to throw a glass decanter at the wall."

Harriet hadn't thought of that. There were people she got upset with and events that made her angry, but there weren't many things that could make her upset enough to throw something. In fact, she couldn't remember a single time she had ever done so. "So who does Lord Beresford care enough about to spark that kind of reaction?"

Daisy laughed. "I can think of exactly two people. Do you know if the police have spoken to Liam's sons?"

"I believe they have," Harriet said. "I reached out to them as well. Stuart wrote back to say that all the questions about his missing father were messing up his schedule."

"He did not." Her tone was incredulous.

"I'm paraphrasing, but that was the gist."

"That boy." Daisy shook her head. "Anything from Eddie?"

"I haven't heard from him. Maybe the police have."

Daisy didn't say anything, but her countenance made it clear there was plenty on her mind.

"What about Lord Beresford's brother?"

"Peter?" Daisy raised an eyebrow. "I don't think Liam has much of a relationship with him, to be honest. They're very different, even in their appearances. Liam is all angles, sharp and quick-witted and dark-haired, and Peter is jolly and outgoing and favors their mother. I can't say Peter couldn't inspire such a strong reaction, but it seems unlikely to me."

How sad it must be for Liam to have strained relationships with his closest family. It was no wonder he was said to be moody and unhappy all the time.

"Have you tried using Coleridge?" Daisy asked.

"Using Coleridge how?"

"To follow the scent trail," Daisy said as if it was the most logical thing in the world. Once she said it, Harriet realized it probably was.

"You mean have Coleridge sniff something of Liam's and track the scent?"

"Yes. I imagine it might be hard right around the house, since the smell of Liam should be all over it, but Coleridge might be able to find the latest scent trail and follow it."

Harriet couldn't believe she hadn't thought of that, especially since the dog had led her and Aunt Jinny to the coat. Why hadn't it occurred to her to take the next step? Now that Daisy pointed it out, it was so obvious. Bloodhounds had been bred specifically to track. Police used them to find missing people sometimes. And here she had a missing person and a bloodhound.

She handed the puppy back to Daisy. "I'll call the police right away to see if they want to use Coleridge to try to find Lord Beresford."

CHAPTER FOURTEEN

As soon as Harriet got into her car, she called Van and explained the idea.

"He's a bloodhound. Purebred by the way, confirmed with the breeder. So my dognapping theory is still a possibility. Bloodhounds are used to track missing people in police investigations sometimes. It's kind of embarrassing that I didn't think of it sooner."

"We've never done something like that around here," Van said. "At least, not in the time I've been a detective constable. I'll have to check with DI McCormick."

"All right. I have some time to bring Coleridge by later today if you want."

"I'll get back to you as soon as I can."

The line went dead. It hadn't gone exactly as she'd thought it would, but hopefully he'd call her soon.

As Harriet drove to the clinic, she mulled over the conversation with Daisy, thinking through the implications of what she'd said. Was one of Lord Beresford's children somehow responsible for the scene in the study? If so, why hadn't they said something to the police when asked about their father?

Stuart was in Canada—or at least he was supposed to be. Harriet wondered if the police had verified that. Edward lived in London.

He could easily have come up to Yorkshire to visit his father. Perhaps something had happened between them to make Lord Beresford leave. Where had he gone so suddenly? If it was sudden. He could have had a trip planned and simply not told Mrs. Lewis. Maybe he'd planned to be back before she came to work on Monday. If that was the case, something had gone terribly wrong.

She wondered if there was a way to find out whether one of his sons—presumably Edward, given his proximity, but Stuart was possible too—had come to see him. Mrs. Lewis said they both had keys to the house. They might have come and gone without anyone outside the house knowing. And if someone had seen such a thing, they wouldn't question a dutiful son visiting his father.

Harriet was nearly back at the clinic when Van called her. "I spoke with the inspector, and she says she'll look into getting the dogs from the regional office involved."

"So she doesn't want to use Coleridge?"

"She can't. If we use dogs, which doesn't happen very often, they have to be specially trained police dogs. It was a good idea though. Thanks for passing it along."

It was a good idea, and Harriet thought it might help to have more noses on the case. Coleridge had already led them to the jacket on the beach. Who knew what he might lead them to if they put him to work? No dog knew Liam Beresford's scent better than Coleridge. But she kept that thought to herself.

"By the way, we looked into that man from Leeds who sent the letters, Leon Evans. He has a solid alibi—was visiting his mum all last weekend after she'd had surgery."

"So he probably didn't have anything to do with Lord Beresford's disappearance?"

"Probably not. But we'll be talking to him more about the letters he's been sending."

"Thanks, Van. Sorry it wasn't a big break for you."

"Hey, every bit helps," he told her.

Harriet hung up. *Every bit helps, huh?* The police couldn't use Coleridge to try to track Lord Beresford, but that didn't mean she couldn't. She called Mrs. Lewis.

"Hello, Harriet. Any news?"

"Not on my end," Harriet said. "It's possible the police know something, but if they do, they haven't told me."

"That's too bad. I was hoping…" Mrs. Lewis trailed off.

"Me too," Harriet said. "Actually, I wanted to ask you something. I was talking with Daisy Lyons—"

"You met Daisy?"

"I did. She's a breeder, and since I'm a vet, I wanted to ask her a few questions—"

"What did she say? Has she seen Lord Beresford?"

"She hasn't," Harriet said. "But she did give me an idea. I was thinking I could have Coleridge sniff around the study, since we know the baron was there recently, and see where he leads us from there. Is there any chance I could come by Beresford Manor with Coleridge later?"

"All right. I haven't gone in today because it seems a bit silly, cleaning and cooking for nobody. But I can go by the house later. I thought the computer shop would have my laptop ready to pick up, but since they don't, I'm free this afternoon. Would you want to meet there at, say, four?"

Harriet went through the afternoon's appointments in her head. "That works for me."

"I'll see you then." Mrs. Lewis hung up.

When Harriet got back to the clinic, Polly looked up from the computer screen, her eyes wide. "Have you seen this?"

"Seen what?"

"The website of the *Whitby Gazette*. They're saying Lord Beresford killed someone and fled the country. It was published this morning."

"I didn't even know they had a website."

"They don't usually break stories like this on the site. Then again, there aren't often stories like this around here. Look."

Harriet leaned in to read the screen and groaned when she saw the headline.

New Evidence Suggests Missing Lord Fled
After Potential Murder

Newly discovered evidence suggests that the Baron Beresford, who was discovered missing on Monday morning, has fled the area or perhaps the country. A source with inside knowledge of the case confirms that the baron's study was found in complete disarray, splattered with blood, and that the baron's purebred bloodhound was found running loose and neglected in the streets of White Church Bay.

Earlier reports that a coat belonging to the baron was found on the beach below a crumbled cliff have proven to be a dead end, as the coat was not in the baron's possession at the time of his disappearance. The identity of the person wearing the coat and how it ended up on the beach below the broken cliff remains unexplained. Sources also confirm that the baron had recently researched destinations overseas.

Representatives from White Church Bay police force declined to be interviewed for this story.

"This is crazy," Harriet said. There were elements of the truth in the article, but it was sensationalized and blown way out of proportion. The byline under the headlines simply read *Staff*—but it had to be Gemma. Who else would have known about "destinations overseas"? And about the coat not being Lord Beresford's? But how could Gemma have included those details? She had assured Harriet she wouldn't print them.

"You're telling me. Do you think that's what really happened? That he offed someone and fled?"

"No, I don't think that's what happened," Harriet said, hearing her own sharp tone and unable to soften it. "Not at all. The article doesn't even support that. It's an inflammatory headline with no evidence. It's irresponsible that they would print something like that. How can they get away with it?"

"Whoever did this was very careful with their wording," Polly said. "Anyway, Doreen Danby is in Room One. Spaghetti, her son's border collie, has a hurt paw."

"Spaghetti?"

Polly smiled. "The kids named the dog."

Harriet chuckled in spite of herself. "Cute." As she walked down the hall, she tried to forget about the article and about the realization that Gemma had printed the information after promising not to. She tried to focus on the border collie, and the pet turtle and cat she saw after, but the situation continued to stew in the back of her mind.

As soon as the last patient left, Harriet picked up her phone and called Gemma.

"Hi, Harriet," Gemma said. "How are you? Is there any news about Lord Beresford? Want to go get dinner?"

Harriet was even more aghast by the reporter's cheerful tone. "Gemma, I saw the article on the *Whitby Gazette* website. How could you print that stuff?"

"The article is getting so much attention," Gemma gushed. "The editors are thrilled. And maybe it'll turn up someone who knows what happened to the baron."

"The things I told you were supposed to be kept quiet."

"It's fine. Most of it is common knowledge at this point anyway."

"What? No, it isn't. Gemma, you agreed that it was all off the record. How could you go ahead and print it anyway?"

"I didn't mention you or quote you, like I promised. I won't tell anyone that you were my source, Harriet."

"You said it was off the record," Harriet protested. "That means you won't print anything from the conversation at all."

Gemma laughed. "No, it means I won't name my source, and I didn't."

"But that's not what off the record means. No part of an off-the-record conversation is supposed to be used."

"That's a common misconception, Harriet." Gemma's voice lost a bit of its upbeat tone. "When a journalist interviews someone off the record, it means that they won't reveal who told them the information, but it's fine to print."

"What? Really?" Harriet's mind spun.

"Of course. I never would have used it otherwise. I would never betray a friend like that. So, do you want to get dinner?"

Harriet felt like she'd been punched in the stomach. Even if Gemma was technically following the rules of journalism, she had cultivated Harriet's friendship for one reason and one reason only. To get an inside scoop on Lord Beresford's disappearance. No matter what she said, Gemma had betrayed her. And now she wanted to go out again, no doubt to pump Harriet for more information.

"No, I don't want to get dinner."

"Aw, too bad. What about tomorrow?"

"I don't think so, Gemma."

"You're not upset, are you? It's standard journalistic practice. I thought you knew that."

"I'm sorry, Gemma. I have to go." Harriet ended the call. Part of her felt bad for effectively hanging up on the reporter, but—but no, actually, she didn't feel bad. She was sure Gemma had only been using her to get a story.

She opened a browser on her phone and searched the phrase *off the record*. Sure enough, the term did mean something different than she'd always thought. If a journalist agreed to the terms, they could print the information revealed in an off-the-record conversation but couldn't attribute the source. There were journalists who felt that it meant full confidentiality, but apparently that was up to their own discretion, and Gemma was among those who stuck to the legal definition.

Harriet felt like an idiot. She'd honestly thought Gemma had been hanging out with her because she liked her. She should have known something was up when Gemma knew the year she'd graduated high school. Gemma had done research on her to get in her good graces. She knew about Dustin and the breakup if she'd seen what was on Harriet's social media. She knew exactly how to get Harriet to trust her.

As upset as she was, it was time to take Coleridge to meet Mrs. Lewis, so she cleaned up the office and locked up then saw Polly off. She let Maxwell and Charlie into the house and made sure they were fed and taken care of. Then she loaded Coleridge into the car and headed for Beresford Manor once again.

Harriet was still miserable when she drove into the driveway of the manor. Coleridge pressed his nose against the glass and wagged his tail as they neared the house. Mrs. Lewis's vehicle was already parked in front, and she sat inside it, talking on her phone. She smiled when she spotted Harriet and climbed out of her car. Harriet let Coleridge out, and he pulled her across the drive toward the front door, his nose to the ground as if declaring his eagerness to work.

"Hello." Mrs. Lewis took a set of keys out of her pocket. "Shall we?"

"Come on, Coleridge."

The dog obeyed, though he kept his nose down. Mrs. Lewis unlocked the heavy front door, and they stepped into the great hall again. The house was still and quiet, and the air felt heavy. Coleridge sniffed his way through the house, pausing to smell things every few feet as Mrs. Lewis led them into the study.

"I'm not sure what would be best for Coleridge to sniff," Mrs. Lewis said. "Maybe the sweater Lord Beresford keeps on the back of his desk chair?"

"That's a good idea," Harriet said. She led Coleridge over to the chair and noticed that the leather-bound book sat alone on the desk.

"Is that his diary?" Harriet asked. Both Daisy and Mrs. Lewis had mentioned that the baron always recorded his appointments in his diary.

"That's right. The police flipped through it but didn't think it had anything important."

"Do you mind if I take a look?"

"Have at it."

Harriet led Coleridge to the sweater and dropped the leash to let him investigate then picked up the diary. It was a handsome leather book, engraved with the initials *LB* in gold. She opened it and gently flipped through the creamy pages. The left-hand pages showed a weekly calendar, and on the right side was room for notes. Various appointments and notes were recorded throughout in pen.

She continued looking until she came to the current week. Then she thumbed back, expecting to see the first week of July.

She stopped. "There's a page missing."

"What?"

She pressed the book open to see the rough edge of the page that had been ripped out, quite close to the spine, and neatly enough that it wasn't obvious at first glance. But when she looked closely, it was clear enough.

"See?" She showed it to Mrs. Lewis.

The housekeeper flipped a page in each direction. "Well, that's strange," she said. "Why would he do that?"

It was a very good question. "Perhaps because he didn't want anyone to see what he'd written there. Or maybe he'd written something he needed to take with him."

"I wonder what it was," Mrs. Lewis said, echoing Harriet's thoughts.

Harriet ran her fingers over the page behind the missing one. She could feel indents in the paper, marks from writing on earlier pages. She held it up to the light, but couldn't make out anything.

"What about doing a rubbing?" Mrs. Lewis said. "Like they do in those old detective shows."

"You mean with a pencil?"

"Exactly. I have no idea if it would work, but maybe it's worth trying?"

Harriet was dubious, but Mrs. Lewis was already pulling a small notebook and a pencil out of the top desk drawer. She ripped a piece of paper out of the notebook, Harriet set the diary on the desk, and Mrs. Lewis laid the lined paper over the missing page. She used the side of the pencil to shade across the surface. At first, all that became visible was rows of graphite piling up, and Harriet was convinced their effort was a waste of time. But then, something appeared. A section of white amidst the graphite.

"What's that?" Mrs. Lewis asked.

"I can't tell yet."

As the housekeeper continued to darken the page, lines began to take shape. When she finished, Harriet was as confused as ever.

MBR DAR KGX 318

"What is that?" Mrs. Lewis asked.

"Maybe 3:18 is a time, but I can't begin to guess what the rest of it means. I think we should probably let the detective constable know."

"You're probably right." Mrs. Lewis made the call and explained what they had found to Van. When she hung up, she told Harriet, "They'll come soon. They're finishing up an appointment."

Harriet thought about what to do next. Should they wait for the police? Or, since it sounded like they had some time, maybe they should do what they had come there to do.

"I think Coleridge is about ready to go." Harriet picked up the sweater and held it in front of him for a good sniff. Was there some signal she was supposed to give him to let him know what she wanted him to do? Maybe this was why the police dogs were preferred for an investigation. They were trained to work on command. But when she pulled the sweater back, Coleridge put his nose to the ground and started sniffing. Harriet dropped the sweater onto the desk, grabbed the leash, and followed him.

He sniffed his way out of the study and into the library, making several detours to check out corners and various scent trails that apparently led nowhere. Harriet was beginning to lose hope that this would produce any kind of useful clue. The baron had been all over his own home. Naturally Coleridge smelled him everywhere.

But eventually, Coleridge sniffed his way to the front door. Out in the gravel drive, he pulled on the leash. Harriet followed, letting him lead. Soon he led her across the parking area and toward the driveway.

"How far are you going?" Mrs. Lewis called.

"I have no idea," Harriet said. "But he appears to have caught a trail. I'm going to let him explore while we're waiting for the police."

"Okay. I'll wait here."

Nose pressed to the ground, Coleridge all but dragged Harriet down the long gravel drive. Could he really be following the baron's scent? Harriet didn't know how long he'd been missing, but it could have been as much as a week since he'd last been at this house. She had no idea how many people had come and gone in that time. Could the dog still smell his master after so long?

But as her feet crunched over the gravel, Harriet wondered. Dogs were motivated by many things—instincts and food being obvious ones. But she thought about a dog trainer she'd known back home. Sandy had always said that more than anything else, dogs wanted their owners' approval, which was why they could be trained to do so many different things. At the end of the day, they were motivated by love as much as anything else, if not more. Could Coleridge be leading her to the master he loved?

When Harriet and Coleridge reached the end of the driveway, she glanced over her shoulder. She couldn't see the house from there, but she was willing to bet Mrs. Lewis was still in the parking area. Coleridge pulled at the leash again, straining to reach a white spot on the ground.

Harriet moved closer and saw that the spot was actually a torn and muddy business card. She picked it up and managed to make out the words *Fletcher Taxi Service*. The address and phone number were illegible.

Harriet pulled out her phone and typed the name into her browser. A second later she hit the call button.

"Hello, Fletcher Taxi Service," said a man's voice. "Where are you and where do you want to go?"

Harriet was momentarily speechless at the bluntness of the question. Then she said, "I'm sorry, I don't need a ride. I was just curious. I believe a friend of mine took a taxi somewhere, and I'm hoping to talk to the person who drove him there."

"Where would your friend have been picked up?"

"Beresford Manor."

He let out a laugh. "Fancy friend."

"Do you know anyone who made a pickup there in the past week or so?"

"I don't," he said. "But I can ask around. Could be one of my mates drove him."

"Would you? That would be wonderful."

"Sure thing. I'll ask around. Give me your number, and I'll give you a call if someone remembers picking up a rider from the big house."

Harriet hesitated. She didn't know this guy from Adam. Should she really give him her number? But then, how could he help her if he didn't have a way to get back to her?

She would have to risk it. She gave him her cell phone number. After all, this was small-town Yorkshire, not New York City.

"And what's your name?" he asked.

"Harriet."

"I'm Tony. I'll ring you if anyone remembers picking up your friend."

"Thank you."

Harriet ended the call and rubbed Coleridge's ears. "Good work, boy. You just got us one step closer to knowing where your master is."

CHAPTER FIFTEEN

Harriet had just reached the house when she heard the sound of a car approaching. She met DI McCormick and Van as they exited the vehicle.

The inspector nodded at Harriet. "I don't know if you saw the article on the *Whitby Gazette*'s website today."

"I did." Harriet ducked her head.

"It contained some information that wasn't meant to be made public. We can't figure out who would have had all those details to share except you." She didn't say it unkindly, but Harriet still felt caught, like a bug pinned to a display.

"We've got people ringing the station saying they've seen Lord Beresford roaming the streets with a bloody knife and all kinds of crazy things," Van said.

"What?" Harriet couldn't understand that.

"People read something like that, and their imagination gets the best of them," DI McCormick said. "Which is why it's so important not to leak private information to the press."

"I'm sorry," Harriet said. "I didn't—" How could she explain how dumb she'd been? "I thought I was talking to a friend. I thought she agreed that she wouldn't print it. I didn't mean to cause problems."

"Just be more careful in the future," said Van.

"I will," Harriet assured them. She held up the business card Coleridge had found. "Coleridge led me to the end of the driveway, and this card was on the ground there. Maybe Lord Beresford really did just go somewhere on his own without telling anyone."

DI McCormick took the card from her and studied it, frowning. "We'll follow up on this. Thank you, Dr. Bailey."

Van and DI McCormick dismissed her then went inside to meet with Mrs. Lewis about the diary. Harriet wearily loaded Coleridge into the Land Rover and headed home. She fed the animals and made herself a simple dinner of baked chicken with a side salad. Her phone rang just as she was finishing up. Gemma's name flashed on the screen.

Harriet took a deep breath and clicked on the answer button. "Hello?" she said.

"Hi, Harriet," Gemma said. "Listen, I know you're upset with me, and I just wanted to let you know how sorry I am. I thought you understood what 'off the record' meant, but that doesn't excuse me for pursuing your friendship to get a story. I wanted you to know that I might have started out that way, but by the end of our first meeting, I truly did want to be friends."

Her tone rang with such sincerity, Harriet believed her. "I appreciate that, Gemma," she said. "Can we chalk it up to a misunderstanding and begin again?"

"I would love that," Gemma said, her voice a bit wobbly.

"Me too," Harriet said. "Just leave your reporter persona home next time, okay?"

"It's a deal." Gemma laughed. "I promise."

They chatted for a few more minutes before they said goodbye, and Harriet ended the call. She was just putting her dishes in the dishwasher when there was a knock at the door.

"Hello?" Aunt Jinny called.

"Hi, Aunt Jinny. Come on in."

Her aunt stepped inside. "It's a nice night. I read the article, and I wondered if you wanted to go for a walk."

Harriet pushed herself up. "Let me grab my sweater." She washed her plate and set it to dry, then she grabbed Coleridge's leash and they started out.

"You were right," Harriet said after a few moments. "About Gemma."

"I didn't want to be," Aunt Jinny said. "I'm here to see how you're doing. It must have been a blow."

"It was at first, but she just called and apologized," Harriet said. "Part of our misunderstanding was my fault, so we're going to try again. But don't worry—I won't be giving her any more scoops for the paper."

"That's good."

Harriet took in a deep breath and let it out slowly. "I'm supposed to have dinner with Claire tomorrow."

"I think you'll be pleasantly surprised."

Though Harriet had been dismissive of Claire before, she started to hope that Aunt Jinny was right.

"How did your visit with Daisy go?" Aunt Jinny asked, changing the subject.

Harriet told her aunt about the visit to Daisy, and then to the manor house, as well as the seemingly random string of letters and numbers they'd found in the diary.

"What in the world does that mean?" Aunt Jinny asked.

"I have no idea. But after I had Coleridge sniff around the study, I let him loose to follow the scent, and he found a business card of a taxi service at the end of the driveway."

"What?"

She filled her aunt in, and by the time they got back to the house, Harriet was in better spirits. Maybe they were finally getting closer to bringing Liam home after all.

CHAPTER SIXTEEN

Harriet woke early on Friday morning. After feeding Charlie and the dogs and letting Maxwell into the yard, she took Coleridge for a walk. As they strolled along the gravel path, past the stone wall, she kept her eyes peeled for any signs of the man who had been hanging around. Fortunately, there were none, which freed her to mull over what she knew about Lord Beresford's disappearance.

His suitcase was gone, and it seemed like he had gotten a ride to somewhere. He could have gone to an airport, a train station, or a bus station, and then he could have gone anywhere in the world. But he was widely considered to be a recluse and never really traveled, and he hadn't told anyone of his plans, not even the housekeeper who cleaned and cooked for him.

He had left his beloved purebred dog without someone to watch over him, and the scene in his study indicated that he had struggled with someone. Daisy had suggested he had a troubled relationship with his sons and that they might be worth looking into.

Harriet was sure the police were doing that. But her mind kept going around and around, and only one thing made sense. He'd left town suddenly, unexpectedly. Whatever the reason, it had followed shortly after he'd had a visitor to Beresford Manor.

Had the visitor been one of his sons? If so, Edward seemed the most likely, since London was much closer than Toronto. And if Edward had visited and had a quarrel with his father, where was Lord Beresford now? Was he still alive? Liam Beresford had last been seen a full week ago. She knew with every day that passed, the chances of finding him alive grew slimmer. Then again, if he'd left of his own accord, as a trip in a taxi indicated, was his safety still a concern?

Harriet returned to the house, feeling more defeated than before. She ate breakfast and read her devotions, asking God to bless her work and the people she encountered that day and asking that Lord Beresford would be brought home safely, and soon.

Then she got ready for the day. She didn't have any farm visits that morning, so she went over to the clinic and did some paperwork before a steady stream of patients came in. She gave an adorable marmalade kitten his shots, treated a bullmastiff's ear mites, and examined a two-year-old goldendoodle's rash.

"We think he must have rolled in something," Gus's owner told her. "We really do try to keep him from doing that, since he seems to have delicate skin."

"It's what dogs do, I'm afraid." Harriet rubbed the soft curly fur on Gus's head. "Give him these pills, and he'll feel better soon."

Harriet was about to see a cat who'd recently started limping when the clinic door burst open and Aunt Jinny blew in. Her hair was blown about by the wind, and she was out of breath. She wore the white lab coat she always wore when she saw patients.

Aunt Jinny should be at the clinic at this time of day. "What's wrong?" Harriet asked.

"King's Cross," Aunt Jinny said. "KGX."

"What?"

"King's Cross train station in London. And MBR is Middlesbrough. Darlington is DAR. I *knew* I'd heard those letters before. I thought about them all morning, trying to unearth what they meant. Then, in the middle of writing a prescription, it came to me. King's Cross is one of the central train stations in London. If Liam had written LHR and we thought he'd taken an airplane, I would have gotten Heathrow airport right away. I'm less familiar with train stations though."

"You're saying he took a train to Middlesbrough, then Darlington, and then from there to London?"

"Exactly. I looked it up. You can take a train from Whitby to Middlesbrough, transfer to Darlington, and then from Darlington to London in about five hours. That route doesn't run on Sunday, but it does on Saturday."

"What's 318?"

"The train number he had to catch at Darlington to get to London. It left Saturday at 3 p.m."

"Okay." Harriet thought this through, trying to make sense of it all. "Two transfers sure seems like a lot. There isn't a more direct route?"

"Not by train. You could drive, but then what would you do with your car when you got to London? You couldn't pay me to drive in London."

"Good point." Harriet didn't relish the idea herself.

"Most people take the train from here," Aunt Jinny said. "It's not that bad, unless you've got tons of luggage."

"So he probably took a taxi to Whitby and the train to London," Harriet said. "But then where did he go?"

"Your guess is as good as mine," Aunt Jinny said. "But I wanted to let you know what I figured out."

"That's awesome," Harriet said. "Thank you so much."

"I should get back now." Aunt Jinny turned and stepped outside and pulled the door closed behind her. Through the window, Harriet saw her hurrying toward her clinic.

"She's a smart one, your aunt," Polly said. "Do you think Lord Beresford went to London?"

"It seems likely," Harriet said. "Now we just need to figure out where he went after that."

Edward's home was a possibility. Daisy had suggested his sons might have had something to do with this. Harriet wished she could race down to London herself and see if he was there, but she knew she had to leave it to the police.

She called Van again. "London," she said as soon as he picked up. "He took a taxi to the train station and then went to London."

"Yes, we figured out the train station codes," Van said.

Harriet felt like a deflating balloon.

"London PD sent officers to the older son's place, and there's no sign of him. Nothing to indicate that the baron is there or has been, and Edward claims he doesn't know a thing about his father's whereabouts. The neighbors haven't seen anyone unexpected around, and there's nothing suspicious about Edward's movements or those of his wife. Everything seems to indicate the baron's not there."

"But where else would he be?" Harriet tried to keep the disappointment from her voice.

"We're following up with the younger son in Canada. He's already told us he doesn't know anything, but we're trying to call in some favors to see if the Toronto PD can help."

"Liam could be in Canada, I guess," Harriet said. By this point, he could be anywhere in the world.

"We're also trying to get ahold of the baron's younger brother to see if he knows anything. But so far, no luck. He doesn't seem to have a landline, and he's not answering his mobile phone. The London PD has been by several times, but there's no answer at the door."

She tried to imagine the chances of finding one missing person in a city the size of London. "He could be anywhere."

"We'll keep searching, Harriet," he said. "But please don't share any of this with your reporter friend, okay?"

"I won't," Harriet promised.

"Glad to hear it."

Harriet hung up, unsettled. Why had Lord Beresford suddenly dashed off to London? She focused on the animals in her care, but for the rest of the afternoon, she was distracted between appointments. For once, closing time was a relief. She said goodbye to Polly and took Maxwell and Charlie and Coleridge back to her place. Impulsively, she snapped on Coleridge's leash. She had to get ready for dinner at Claire's soon, and Aunt Jinny had offered to watch him this evening, but she had time for a short walk to clear her head.

She was halfway to the cliff path when her phone rang. It was an unfamiliar local number. Then again, most of the local numbers were unfamiliar to her.

"Hello, this is Dr. Bailey."

"Hi, this is Owen. I'm a taxi driver in the area. Are you the lady who asked about the pickup at Beresford Manor?"

"That's right," Harriet said.

"My coworker, Tony, gave me your number. I made that pickup at the manor and took him to the Whitby train station last Saturday. That's quite a house."

"It is indeed." Harriet couldn't believe it. Someone had actually called her. "Did Lord Beresford tell you where he was headed, or why?"

"Nah, he wasn't chatty. I tried to engage him—you get better tips if they like you—but he didn't want to talk about it, or anything else, really. Some people are like that. He tipped well enough anyway."

"He didn't say if he was going to visit someone, or if he was on holiday?"

"Nope. Didn't say. But man, what a house."

"It is a nice house," Harriet agreed.

"The garden is something else too. I've never seen a garden like that, everything planted in neat rows and the hedges all clipped perfectly. It's like something from another century."

"Wait. You saw the garden?" The garden was behind the house, on the back side of the property. "How did you see that when you picked up Lord Beresford?"

"Ah, I didn't see it when I picked him up. It was the other time. I've been driving taxis around here for nearly ten years and never been to that house, but then suddenly I was there twice in two days."

"You were there twice?" She'd reached the cliff walk, and below her, the waves pounded against the sand as the tide came in. She strained to hear him.

"Yeah. The first time was on Friday, the day before I picked up the older man. A bloke got off the train in Whitby and asked me to drive him to the house. I'd never been there, so I was happy to see it. Then he asked me to stick around and wait because he didn't plan to stay long and didn't want to have to wait for another taxi to come all the way out. He promised to pay me for my time, so I agreed. But I got bored waiting in the cab, so I wandered around some to check out the grounds. Figured it was probably the only time in my life I'd get that close to a house that grand."

Harriet's mind raced, trying to keep up with the information he'd revealed. "Do you know who the man was?"

"He didn't say, and he paid in cash. But I got the sense he knew the place well. He walked in like he owned the place when he arrived."

"Did he mention where he was from, or why he was going to the house?"

"Nah. The men at that house aren't a chatty bunch. But I guessed London. He had that hoity-toity accent and the posh clothes. People in London dress differently, you know? He wore tailored trousers and a sweater made of some really nice material."

"What did he look like?"

"Skinny, but not like he worked out. Posh clothes, like I said. Ginger hair and beard."

"He had red hair?"

"Flaming orange."

Edward lived in London and had red hair and a beard.

"How long was he in the house?" she asked.

"About an hour. I scrolled on my phone for a while, but that's only interesting for so long. So I got out and walked around. Enjoyed the garden. There was a stable, but I didn't see any horses."

Harriet turned back toward the house.

"And when the red-haired man came out of the house, how did he seem?"

"Oh, he had a monk on. What you'd call angry. I don't know what happened in there, but it didn't go well. He got in the car, demanded to be taken back to the station, and sat there staring out the window, but you could see on his face he was upset."

"Did he mention why?"

"Nope. Like I said, they're not a chatty bunch. But he paid me well, so I was happy."

"Did he seem okay, generally?" She thought about the blood. "Not, I don't know, injured or something?"

"Injured? Not that I could tell. Why would he be?"

Instead of answering, she asked, "Is there anything else you remember about either man?"

"Afraid not."

"Thank you. I appreciate your call and the information."

Harriet hung up. It must have been Edward who had shown up last Friday. They'd quarreled, and on Saturday Lord Beresford had unexpectedly taken a train to London and hadn't been seen since. Why had he gone? Where was he now? What had happened to him in London?

Harriet's thoughts were interrupted by sudden loud barks from Coleridge. He strained against the leash, pulling toward the house. She looked to see what had gotten his attention—and froze.

The curly-haired man leaned against his silver car, arms crossed over his chest, waiting for them.

CHAPTER SEVENTEEN

Coleridge yanked against the leash and let out another series of sharp barks.

Harriet expected the man to run away as he had both times she'd seen him lurking around the house, but today he wasn't lurking. Or running away. Harriet grabbed for her phone, hands shaking. With one hand, she tried to hold Coleridge back, and with the other, she attempted to call Van.

Slowly, the man raised his hand. Was he...waving? She tried to make out the expression on his face, but he was too far away to say for sure whether it was a grimace or a smile. Coleridge still strained against the leash, forcing her to put her phone back in her pocket and use both hands to keep him from bolting. Uncertainly, she followed his lead across the yard, waiting for the man to run away again, but he stayed.

"It's all right," he called as they reached the edge of the gravel parking area. "I'm not going to hurt you."

That wasn't as reassuring as he probably meant it to be.

"Hey, Coleridge." The dog was still barking, still pulling at the leash. "Did you miss me, buddy?"

Harriet let go of the leash, and Coleridge ran to the man, dancing around him with his tongue lolling out in canine joy.

"Who's a good boy? Did you miss me?" He crouched down to return the dog's greeting then straightened and held out a hand to Harriet. "Trey Casey."

"Harriet Bailey." She shook his hand uncertainly. "How do you know Coleridge? What are you doing here?"

"I'm sorry if I scared you before."

Up close, she could see that he had pale skin and freckles, with deep creases around his eyes and mouth.

"I shouldn't have run away," he continued. "I was afraid, but I shouldn't have—"

"*You* were afraid?" Harriet said. "You skulked around my property and then ran off when you got caught, not once but twice. What in the world were you afraid of?"

"I'm so sorry. I didn't mean—" He rubbed Coleridge's ears, as if trying to come up with the words. "Let me explain."

"You have two minutes before I call the cops." She grabbed her phone again.

"Okay. So last Saturday morning, I was at home, working on my car, when this car pulls into my driveway. I recognized it right away, of course. Not too many Bentleys around here. I live in one of the cottages on the property, so obviously I know who Lord Beresford is, though I've never spoken to him before. I don't think he knew who I was. Don't know why he chose me, except that I was the closest and I was home."

He lived in one of the old laborer's cottages on the manor house property. Things were starting to fall into place.

"Chose you for what?"

"He got out, told me he had to leave town, and asked if I could take care of his dog for a few days."

"He didn't know you, but he asked you to take care of his dog?"

"You think it sounds strange? Imagine how I felt. I have a cat. I don't know what to do with a huge dog. But what was I supposed to say? If the lord of the manor shows up and asks you to care for his dog, you don't refuse."

"You don't work for him, do you?"

"Nah, I'm an electrician. I rent the place. But still, it's not like I could have said no, is it?"

Harriet let it go. "Did he say why he wanted you to care for his dog?"

"Aside from having to leave town, no. Didn't say when he was coming back, or ask whether I had any plans of my own, or if I wanted to care for a dog. Didn't even ask for my name until the very end. He handed me his dog on a leash, a bottle of some kind of medicine, and a bag of food. He said he'd be in touch soon."

Harriet's mind reeled. If Trey had told the police about this visit days ago, it would have saved a lot of worry, expense, and hassle. If they'd known on Monday that the baron had made arrangements— crude as they were—for the dog while he was away, it would have changed everything.

"But why would he do that?" Harriet offered boarding services, as her grandfather had. It wasn't as if Lord Beresford didn't know about the vet practice. He'd been taking Coleridge there since he was a puppy. And he must have known that Daisy would happily dog-sit as long as he needed her to.

"Got me. All I can say is that he seemed very distracted. Like he wasn't all there, you know? At the time, I thought nothing of it. A man like that never has to think about whether what he's asking is crazy. He does what he wants, and everyone else falls in line. He wants you to take care of his dog, you do it. So I took the dog, and we spent the rest of Saturday and all of Sunday together at my place, waiting for the baron to come back. We had some fun together, didn't we, Coleridge?"

Trey bent over to pet him, and Coleridge licked Trey's face.

So many questions ran through Harriet's mind, fighting for precedence. "So if you were taking care of Coleridge, why was he running loose on Monday?"

"I felt awful about that," he said. "But I wasn't exactly set up to take care of a huge dog, now was I? I don't have a cage, or whatever those things are."

"A crate?"

"That's it. My mum told me afterward that I should have put him in a crate when I had to go out, but I didn't know that, and I didn't have one even if I had known it. But I had to go to work, didn't I? It wasn't like Beresford offered to pay me for my trouble or anything like that. So on Monday I went to work, and I left Coleridge in the house."

Harriet began to see where this was going. "He got out?"

"I don't lock the back door. I never do. No one ever comes down that way, and I didn't know the dog could open doors."

"He opened a door?"

"Mum thinks I must not have closed it all the way. I must not have, and he got out. I came home to find that Lord Beresford's purebred bloodhound was gone, and I knew I was in serious trouble. I asked around and heard he'd been taken in by the new vet. So I came down here to explain Monday night."

"But then you ran away."

"Yeah, I panicked and thought twice about it. I'd lost the baron's dog. I really didn't want anyone to know that."

"The police were looking for you for attempted dognapping. That's what I thought you were doing here."

He gaped at her. "Why would you think that?"

"What was I supposed to think? I had this valuable dog that belonged to a baron. He's valuable on his own, or he could probably be ransomed. Suddenly a man shows up and seems to have an interest in the dog but runs away instead of talking to me, which tells me he's up to no good."

"That explains why I saw the police come by as I left that second time. My mum kept trying to get me to come get him, but I figured he was better off where he was and I could explain to the baron when he got back."

"If you were so convinced he was better off, why did you come here today?"

"Mum just wouldn't let it go," he said, hanging his head. "She said I had to stop being a coward and come forward. Let you know what happened, that the dog wasn't abandoned when Lord Beresford left town. And to give you this."

He held out a bottle. Coleridge's missing medicine. "We figured he must need it."

"I'm glad you did," Harriet said. "But why now? You've had this medicine the whole time, and obviously the dog needs it. And surely you heard Lord Beresford was reported missing earlier this week? It seems very likely that you were the last person to see him. Why didn't you let the police know what had happened?"

"I don't read the papers, so I had no idea. I thought he was still away. He never did tell me exactly how long he planned to be gone. I didn't know that people were saying he was kidnapped, or worse. But when my mum saw the article last night, she said I had to come forward with what I knew."

"I'm glad you came and told me," Harriet said. "But what about the police? Have you told them?"

"Not yet." He scuffed the toe of his boot on the ground. "I know I need to."

"You do. Or else I will."

He nodded. "I'll call them as soon as I get home."

Harriet wanted to insist that he do it now, but she decided to trust he would do it. "So you're really not here to dognap Coleridge?"

"No. He's better off here than with me anyway. Obviously."

At least one part of the mystery was solved. She now knew how Coleridge had ended up loose. And she knew that the baron had left of his own accord. But when would he come back for his dog? He'd told Trey he would only be gone a few days, but that was nearly a week ago.

What had happened to Lord Beresford since then?

CHAPTER EIGHTEEN

Claire lived in a little house a few blocks from Polly, in the upper part of town. The street was lined with small brick cottages, and trees reached leafy branches over the road. Harriet parked on the street in front of the house and walked up the sidewalk, holding a bunch of flowers she'd cut from her garden.

Claire opened the door before she even had a chance to knock. "Hello, Harriet. Come in. So glad you made it. Thanks for coming."

"Thanks for having me," Harriet said.

The living room was dominated by a large sectional sofa that faced the television, and kids' things—backpacks, toys, a portable gaming system—littered every surface.

"Please excuse the mess. I've been asking Desmond to put his cleats away all afternoon, and now I see he never did. I'm sorry about that." She swept a pair of athletic shoes out of the way. "What lovely flowers. Are they from your garden?"

"They are," Harriet said. "Though I can't claim responsibility for them. My grandfather hired a service to take care of the yard and gardens, and I haven't gone another direction yet."

"It's good of you to share those benefits. Let's go put them in water. Everyone is out back." She led Harriet past a staircase. Strips of wallpaper had been peeled off, leaving behind most of the floral print. "Ignore that. Russell got halfway through that project last weekend and then conveniently got distracted. Do you know how hard it is to get wallpaper off?"

Being here was exactly like Harriet had thought it would be—a whirlwind. Claire was always in motion, always doing something. But as Harriet followed her into the small kitchen, it also felt comfortable. She'd expected to feel overwhelmed by Claire's energy, but now that she was here, something in her relaxed. Maybe it was the fact that the house wasn't in immaculate order but Claire didn't seem upset by it. She displayed no need to show off a perfect home or perfect family. Her hair wasn't perfectly done, and she wore an apron with a ketchup stain on it over her jeans and casual top. But Harriet felt truly welcome, as if Claire was genuinely delighted to see her.

"Would you like something to drink?" Claire gestured at a pitcher on the counter, which was filled with the carbonated beverage the British referred to as lemonade. Harriet had learned that they referred to American lemonade as lemon juice or lemon drink.

"That sounds lovely."

"Coming right up. So how are you? How has your week been?"

While Claire took a glass out of a wooden cabinet and poured some lemonade into it, Harriet thought about how to answer. "A bit confusing, to be perfectly honest."

"Welcome to the club." Claire laughed. "It must be totally overwhelming, moving not only to a new place but a whole new country. What's happened? Maybe I can help."

"I appreciate the sentiment," Harriet said. "But unless you know what happened to Lord Beresford, I'm not sure what you can do."

"Oh, that." Claire handed her the glass. "I don't know a thing about it, but I do hope he's found quickly, don't you?"

"More than anything," Harriet said. She probably shouldn't have brought it up. The last thing she needed was another friend spreading information about what she knew. "Anyway, how was your week?"

"It was lovely. The kids are off school for the summer, which is nice," Claire said. "They're old enough to get themselves dressed and fed, and they can take care of themselves while I'm at work. I work mornings in the summer, so I can be around to drive them to various lessons and camps in the afternoon."

"That's nice." Harriet was surprised that Claire had dropped the subject of the baron so easily. It seemed like it was all anyone in town was talking about. And Harriet didn't get the sense Claire wasn't interested in talking about it but rather that she'd understood and respected Harriet's desire to move past the topic. "How do you like working at the church?"

"It's great." She poured a glass for herself, and then she took a vase from the cabinet and filled it with water. "The hours are good, the people are nice, and Pastor Will is great to work with. He's a stand-up man all around."

"I agree with that." Will was the pastor at White Church and a friend of Harriet's.

"Plus, the work is flexible, which is helpful with the kids, and it's nice to do something that feels like it matters, you know?"

Harriet and Claire continued to chat while Claire arranged the flowers, and Harriet felt herself growing more and more relaxed and comfortable by the minute. Then they headed out to the backyard, where Claire introduced her to Russell, her husband, as well as twelve-year-old Desmond and nine-year-old Bella.

Russell shook her hand and welcomed her. "Your grandfather was a great man. We were sorry to lose him."

"But we're very glad you're here," Claire added.

"Well, yes, of course we are." Russell smiled. "When the news came that you would be replacing him—a stranger moving into his home *and* taking over his practice—it was funny to see how many people in town got their knickers in a twist."

"Russell." Claire batted him playfully with a pot holder. "Don't go telling her things like that. We're all so glad you're here, Harriet. Your grandfather talked about how proud he was of you all the time, and it's wonderful to get to know you properly."

Harriet talked to Russell about his job in IT. Desmond challenged her to a game of basketball and was shocked when Harriet sank more hoops than he did. Bella asked her whether she had been to any American theme parks, and when Harriet said she had, Bella asked her about all her favorite rides and games. Then the little girl spent the next ten minutes begging her parents to take her to America.

By the time the fresh-from-the-grill burgers were served, Harriet found herself thinking she'd been completely wrong about Claire. She wasn't put-together or smooth or fashionable—but she was genuine and honest. She was funny and kind, and she seemed eager to get to know Harriet and make her feel welcome in the community.

For the second time that week, Harriet felt like she might have found a friend.

When Harriet pulled into the driveway after a wonderful evening with Claire and her family, she saw that the light in Aunt Jinny's clinic was on. That was odd. Her aunt didn't usually work so late.

Harriet parked her car and sat for a moment. She was tired, and Aunt Jinny probably didn't need her nosing around if she was trying to catch up on work. But it was so unusual to see the light on at that time of night. Harriet decided to poke her head in to see if Aunt Jinny needed anything. If her aunt needed nothing, no harm would be done. But if she did and Harriet didn't offer it, Harriet would feel awful.

She made her way across the gravel drive, her feet crunching on the rocks, the a fresh, cool breeze caressing her cheeks and ruffling her hair.

She knocked gently on the door but didn't hear a response. She tried the doorknob and found it unlocked. She stepped into the small waiting area. The reception desk was empty.

"Aunt Jinny?" Harriet called.

"I'm here!"

Harriet walked down a short hallway, past the exam rooms, and into the office at the back. She found Aunt Jinny hunched over some files on her desk, reading glasses perched on her nose. "Are you still working at this hour?"

"Kind of. I'm trying to make sense of something."

"What do you mean?"

Aunt Jinny took off her reading glasses and set them on her desk. "Remember how I told you the police asked about the blood type of each member of the Beresford family?"

"To check into the blood that was on the decanter," Harriet said. "Have they figured out whose it was yet? Was it Edward's?"

"Edward? Why would you guess that?" Aunt Jinny didn't say whether she was right or wrong, Harriet noted.

"I think it was Edward who was there with him." Harriet explained what she had learned that day.

"His son, is it?" Aunt Jinny murmured. "Well, that would be an interesting wrinkle."

"What do you mean? Was it Edward's blood?"

"Maybe," Aunt Jinny said. She indicated Harriet should take a seat, and Harriet sat down in the empty chair across from her desk.

"Something doesn't make sense," Aunt Jinny said. "Van and DI McCormick came by here tonight to ask me some questions about blood types. Their questions made it clear that the blood they found on the decanter was AB negative."

"Okay." Harriet didn't know everything about human blood types, though she knew all about animal blood types. Dogs alone had seven. "So what does that mean?"

"That's the rarest of all blood types," Aunt Jinny said. "Only about one percent of the population has that blood type."

"That should make it relatively easy to match it to the right person then," Harriet said.

Aunt Jinny hesitated. "Usually I wouldn't share patient information, but I need to talk this out with someone."

Aunt Jinny's professional boundaries were important to her, so if she needed to talk something out with Harriet, it was serious. "My lips are sealed," Harriet promised.

"Liam Beresford is AB negative," Aunt Jinny said. "That information is in our records. So chances are that the blood in the study belongs to him. Blood type is hereditary, so it's possible Edward could also be AB negative. He was never a patient here, so I don't have his records. The boys went to a pediatric clinic in Scarborough before they went off to boarding school."

"If the blood could belong to either Lord Beresford or his son, that lines up with the possibility that it was the two of them in the study," Harriet said. "It seems like they fought about something, and Edward stormed off. Lord Beresford left the next day, though we don't know where he went or why. Or when he's coming back—if he's even planning to at this point."

Aunt Jinny watched her with a worried expression.

"What is it?"

"The thing is, AB negative is a rare enough blood type that it got me wondering about Lord Beresford's parents' blood types. I treated the previous Lord Beresford—Liam's father, Richard—many years ago, when I first started out. His regular doctor, who used to have a clinic in the village, was away on holiday, and I was called in to treat him after a seizure. I was terrified, if you want to know the truth. I was fresh out of medical school and afraid I might make things even worse for the lord of the manor. But it worked out fine. I prescribed some antiseizure medication and ordered some tests, and he was okay until his regular doctor came home. I drew some blood for the tests." She tapped the papers in front of her. "I dug out those old records and discovered that his blood type was O negative."

"That's the universal donor type, right?" Harriet thought she'd seen that on a sign at the last blood drive she'd attended.

"That's right. Anyone can have a transfusion of O negative blood, and it's in high demand for that reason. But the thing is..." She broke off.

Harriet waited for her to go on.

"Genetics can be funny," Aunt Jinny continued. "There are always anomalies, and you can't draw any real conclusions without more investigation."

"What is it, Aunt Jinny?" She'd found something that didn't seem right, that much was clear.

"Like I said, blood type is inherited. Like any other heritable trait, a child receives genes from both parents and ends up with some combination of the genes all its own. But the child should only inherit traits that are coded into the genes."

"Right." So far, Harriet was following.

"The thing is, a parent with O blood should not have a child with AB negative blood," Aunt Jinny said. "To wind up with AB blood, you usually get an A gene from one parent and a B gene from the other. If the father had O type blood, he wouldn't have been able to pass on either."

"You mean, genetically it's impossible?"

"Nothing is impossible. There are always anomalies," Aunt Jinny repeated. "But it would be quite extraordinary. I've spent the past hour poring over the latest research, trying to make sense of this, to see if there's anything that would explain how this would happen." She gestured at her open laptop. "I can't find anything to explain it except for the obvious answers."

"Adoption?" Harriet asked.

"Or an affair."

"What about his mother's blood type? Couldn't he have gotten AB blood from her?"

"O is recessive, so I can see where you're coming from, but no. Even if she was AB, she would have passed on either the A or the B but not both. A father with O negative blood should not be able to produce a child with AB negative blood, regardless of the mother's blood type. Which means that Liam Beresford is a statistical anomaly, a truly rare exception. But the more likely explanation is that—"

"Richard Beresford was not Liam's biological father," Harriet finished for her. She thought about the possibility for a moment before the implications sank in. "Wait. Lord Beresford is an inherited title."

Aunt Jinny nodded. "By law, only biological descendants of the titleholder may inherit. Adopted and illegitimate children have legal protections and can receive courtesy titles as if they were younger siblings, but they cannot inherit the title regardless of their birth order. If it turns out Richard Beresford wasn't Liam's biological father…"

Harriet understood what her aunt was driving at. If that was true, the baron's whole life was a lie. The title, the house—none of it belonged to Liam Beresford. "What if he was adopted all this time, but no one knew?"

"It's possible," Aunt Jinny said. "And I understand why his parents would have hidden that. If it was known that he was adopted, he wouldn't have been able to inherit."

"So we have three possibilities. One, he was adopted and it was kept a big secret," Harriet said. "Two, he's a statistical anomaly."

"There's a very, very small chance of that, but it's not zero," Aunt Jinny added.

"Or three, Richard Beresford was not Liam Beresford's biological father for another reason," Harriet concluded. "Two of those options would mean that he is not actually Lord Beresford. The title, the house—he's not entitled to any of it."

Aunt Jinny bit her lip. "The title, the lands, the house, would all belong to Richard's closest male relative, who would be his rightful heir. Whoever that might be." She sighed. "And if this is true—if Richard Beresford isn't Liam Beresford's biological father—then there are a number of people with a lot to lose."

Liam, for one. Edward, his eldest son and presumptive heir to the title, for another.

"And some people with a lot to gain," Harriet said. "What about the younger brother? Liam's brother, Peter?"

"Whose blood type is A negative, according to my records," Aunt Jinny said. "Which is possible with an O-negative father. It's not proof that he is Richard's biological son. But we can't definitively say he's not."

If Peter was legitimate, he should have inherited everything, not Liam. "Who was Liam's father, if not Richard Beresford?"

"I have no way of knowing that," Aunt Jinny said. "Someone who could have contributed to the genetic makeup for his AB blood."

"Who could have known about this?" Harriet finally asked. "Richard Beresford? Liam himself?"

"I have no idea," Aunt Jinny said. "If the one clue has been buried in these files for so many years, maybe no one. So I've been sitting here, trying to figure out whether to let someone know what I suspect."

Harriet let out a breath. "Normally I would say no, but the fact that the baron is missing under such strange circumstances—I mean, this could be a lead."

Aunt Jinny met her gaze. "It does leave one to wonder, doesn't it?"

CHAPTER NINETEEN

Harriet's mind was still swirling when she made it home that night. If Lord Beresford was not biologically a Beresford, that knowledge would change lives. As archaic as the peerage system seemed to her, it still affected the lives of real people, in very real ways. Had someone found out the truth? How desperately might Lord Beresford have tried to cling to his title, if confronted with the evidence that he could lose everything? How hard might Edward fight to hold on to his promised future?

And what about Liam's brother, Peter? If he could prove that he was the only biological son of Richard Beresford, his life could change in dramatic ways. He would stand to inherit the title and property, which his brother would be forced to forfeit. He had the strongest motive for wanting the truth to come out.

Instead of getting ready for bed, Harriet opened her laptop and typed *Peter Beresford* into the search bar. It didn't take long for her to discover that he was a private-practice lawyer. He lived in a nice area of London called Chelsea. He was married, with one grown son. And all the photos she saw of him showed one outstanding characteristic.

He had red hair. Or had, at one point. It was threaded through with white, but it was still clear that he was a natural ginger. He had a beard as well.

Harriet had assumed that it was Edward who had come to see Liam Beresford, based on the description given by the taxi driver. But could it have been Peter after all, come to claim his title?

Harriet couldn't get her mind to settle and didn't fall asleep until quite late on Friday night, so she slept in on Saturday morning. She finally woke when Charlie, impatient for her breakfast, jumped up on the bed and meowed loudly in her face.

"Okay, I'm coming," she groaned, reaching out to pet the cat. Charlie promptly hopped down off the bed, no doubt to wait by her food bowl.

Harriet dressed, read her morning devotions, and then, after taking the dogs out for a walk, got ready for her day. It was drizzly out, and she was glad to step back inside and dry off. She did some cleaning, made a shopping list, and started a load of laundry. Then she grabbed her purse and notebook and headed into town. She would stop at the grocery store on the way home.

But her first stop was the White Church Bay Library, which was housed in a stone cottage in the upper part of town, with big white shutters on either side of the tall windows that flanked the door. The cottage had previously been a blacksmith's shop, a pub, and even a vacuum retailer, but it had been converted into a quaint place to read and browse. Harriet had already found that the collection of materials on local history was strong, and though the selection of modern books could be limited, they were happy to fill requests through the interlibrary system. The basement held meeting rooms and a row of computer terminals that could be used for research and internet access.

Harriet decided to start by seeing whether the library held any books that might give her some more context and background on the Beresford family. She browsed the local history section and found some promising titles—*A Record of the Peerages of Northern Yorkshire*, *A History of Yorkshire Families*, and an illustrated book called *Manor Houses in Northern Yorkshire*. She carried them to a table and began to leaf through them.

The first book was a record of names for the men who had held various titles throughout the centuries. She found the listing for the Baron Beresford and ran her finger down the names. Liam Beresford had taken over the title from his father, Richard, who'd inherited it from his father, Gregory, who'd inherited from his father… At a few points, the history got a little interesting when the title had passed to a nephew or a cousin for want of a male heir, but other than that, the book told her almost nothing useful.

She set it aside and picked up the book with pictures of manor houses in northern Yorkshire. She found Beresford Manor, which was depicted in lush photographs that highlighted the woodwork, the art collection, and the gardens. If she hadn't already been inside the house a few times, she might have found this more useful, but as pretty as it was, she wasn't sure how any of it helped her.

Harriet opened the book of Yorkshire family histories. Of course, it didn't feature everyday families like her own but rather noble families, including the Beresford family in chapter ten. She skimmed much of the older history and narrowed in on the sections that discussed more recent generations.

Gregory, the eldest child, was said to be a taciturn boy, quiet and interested in mathematics and biology more than business and estate management. He was said to have collected specimens of moths and other insects, neatly labeling them to display in the nursery. Charlotte and Mary, the younger children, were loud and rambunctious, often reprimanded by the governess for unladylike behavior. It was said they enjoyed tormenting their older brother...

Harriet skipped ahead.

Richard Gregory Beresford, the seventeenth Baron Beresford, was born in 1937. He was the third child, born after Wallace, a sickly child who passed away before his first birthday, and Eliza. Richard did well in his schoolwork and excelled in sports, especially polo.

Harriet had never met anyone who played polo. She skimmed ahead until she found what she was looking for.

Richard met Alexandra Clayton at a charity ball and was immediately taken with her. Her auburn hair, fair skin, and blue eyes were enchanting, and her laughter and kind spirit held the future baron in their grasp. Richard was smitten. After a whirlwind courtship of three months, he proposed to Alexandra. The couple were married at White Church in White Church Bay.

Alexandra had attended the ball as a guest of Margaret Kearny, second daughter of the baron of Highsmith, who later married Blake Granger, a friend of both women from their time at Somerville College at Oxford. The two couples were said to be good friends and vacationed together for much of their lives.

Richard and Alexandra's first child, Liam Gregory, was born September 26, 1956, and was joined by Peter Wallace on November 14, 1958. The family lived at Beresford Manor, where Alexandra hosted many community fairs. She also chaired many fundraisers and gatherings in the village. Though the grand manor was kept up during this time, rising costs forced the seventeenth baron to sell off parcels of the property, including the workers' cottages and a hundred acres of farmland, which became part of the National Trust.

Liam Beresford, the eighteenth Baron Beresford, was a dreamy child, always interested in art and architecture more than the business of running an estate...

It went on from there, but Harriet was particularly interested in the friendship between the Beresfords and the Grangers. The bit about the couples being close struck her as an odd detail to include. She should learn more about the Grangers. Skimming the index, she found that this was the sole reference to the Granger family, though there was a whole entry on the Baron of Highsmith. Margaret Granger, née Highsmith, was mentioned in passing as the baron's younger daughter—a role barely even worth commenting on, Harriet had come to understand. Not heir to anything, and a woman at that, Margaret was little more than a footnote in the story of the men around her.

Harriet closed the book and pushed the stack away. She didn't think there was much more she could learn from these books. She placed them on the cart to be reshelved and headed to the corner where the research terminals were located. She sat down at one of the terminals and studied the library's home screen, which listed different avenues for research. She wanted a newspaper archive, or a—

"Need any help?" A woman had joined her. She was in her early fifties, with long black hair threaded with white and pulled into a ponytail.

"How did you guess?"

"You have that look." She smiled. "I'm Adah Singh. I'm one of the librarians here."

"Harriet Bailey."

"You're Doc Bailey's granddaughter, aren't you? I'd heard you moved into his old place."

"That's me. It's great to meet you."

"Your grandfather was a delightful man. We have one of his paintings in our house, and I've never heard anything but good about his skills as a veterinarian," Adah said. "I hope you're enjoying your time here so far."

"Oh yes. Everyone is so welcoming."

"Well, please let me know if there's anything I can help you with as you settle in."

"Thank you." Adah's warm, genuine manner set Harriet at ease. "For now, I'm hoping to locate the newspaper archive."

"Of course. If you click here"—Adah pointed to a tab on the screen—"you'll be able to search any newspaper in the UK and many of the major papers from around the world. If you're looking for a specific newspaper or time frame, you can narrow your search parameters here."

Adah showed Harriet how to search for what she needed then pointed out different archives, genealogy sites, and records databases the library had access to.

"Are you looking for local news?" Adah asked.

"I think so?"

"Do you have a specific time frame?"

Harriet thought for a moment. "The fifties or sixties, probably."

"The *Whitby Gazette* should have what you need. You might check the archives there, though the older records are kind of spotty."

"Thank you. I'll start there."

"Let me know if you need help with anything else." Adah waved and wandered over to help another patron who had sat down in front of a terminal.

Harriet opened the newspaper archive again and narrowed her search to the *Gazette*, at any time, and typed in the name Alexandra Beresford. Several hits came up, mostly from the 1950s, '60s, and '70s. The first link was an article that had been scanned in from a newspaper. It listed Alexandra as one of the hosts of a tea held to raise funds for the creation of a local library in 1972. *Well done, Alexandra.*

The next article showed results from a horse show, where Alexandra was reported to have placed high in dressage, riding a horse called Fletcher. Harriet had loved watching televised dressage competitions when she'd visited her grandfather years ago. The high-stepping horses, the beautiful music, the unimaginable work that had obviously gone into training for both the mount and the rider—it had always fascinated her. She and Grandad always compared their favorites afterward.

She found an obituary from 1975. Alexandra had died of lung cancer and been deeply mourned by her family and friends. There were several mentions of Alexandra hosting fairs at the manor house, several places where she was featured in photographs at charity events. She was beautiful, radiating health and life even in grainy black-and-white photos. Harriet found a photograph of Alexandra in a Jackie O-style suit dress at a tea in 1962 particularly charming.

But the one she found most interesting was a picture of Alexandra in a high-waisted ball gown with cap sleeves and long white gloves from August 1956. Alexandra was noticeably pregnant in the photo, the silky fabric of her gown stretched over her round, high belly. Liam had been born in September 1956, according to the book she'd read earlier.

The timing worked. Harriet sat back. It wasn't conclusive proof, but it did seem to indicate that Liam had been born to Alexandra, which dispelled their suspicion that he was adopted. Unless something really bizarre had happened—babies switched at birth or something—it was fairly obvious that Liam was the child of Alexandra Beresford.

But was he the son of Richard as well, regardless of what his blood type indicated?

Harriet ran a search for *Liam Beresford*, and hundreds of results came up. She narrowed her focus to 1956 and 1957, though she had no idea what she hoped to find. Information about his birth and parentage, she supposed. After digging through several useless articles, Harriet did find something interesting.

The *Gazette* had a story from Liam's christening in the winter of 1957. As the heir to the barony, this was big news, apparently. The paper had run a photo of a baby in a lacy white gown held by the woman Harriet recognized as Alexandra, who stood next to a man she knew to be Richard. Another couple stood with the parents and child. There was no caption under the photo, and when Harriet clicked on the story itself, only the first paragraph came up.

> *The Baron Beresford and his wife, Alexandra, baptized their son, Liam Gregory, on February 17 at White Church in White Church Bay. The heir to the title, Liam was born on September 26, 1956. In attendance at the christening were his godparents...*

The story had dropped off, probably continued on another page, but the second page wasn't included. Who were the godparents? Harriet assumed they must be the other couple in the photo? She checked all the other links that came up, and even searched for *Liam Beresford christening* but wasn't able to find the second part of the story. She went back to the photo and took a picture of it with her phone.

Who was the other couple in the photo?

It was much more than idle curiosity that drove her desire to figure it out.

The man in the photo, presumably Liam's godfather, had the same high cheekbones, the same widow's peak, and the same dimpled chin as Liam had in the photos she'd seen.

Whoever this man was, Harriet thought there was a good chance that he was Liam's biological father.

CHAPTER TWENTY

Harriet continued to stare at the photo of the christening, growing more certain that the other man in the photo was the baron's father. Technically, Liam wouldn't be the baron if she was right. Harriet needed to figure out who the man was.

The thing was, Harriet thought she'd seen the couple before. She couldn't be sure now—perhaps she was projecting what she hoped—but she thought these were the same people she'd seen in the family photographs in the library at Beresford Manor. If the book she'd read earlier was accurate, it was likely that these were the dear friends of Richard and Alexandra, Blake and Margaret Granger. How could she find out for sure if she was right?

She started with an internet search, but their names were common enough that nothing useful turned up. As Harriet thought about the christening photo, the answer suddenly became obvious. The christening had taken place at White Church. The church kept records of things like weddings, funerals, and christenings. She wondered if the names of the godparents were in the church's records as well.

There was one way to find out. Harriet thought about heading over to the church to see if anyone was there and would let her poke around in the records, but then she had a better idea. She pulled out her phone.

"Hello?" Claire was outside somewhere, judging by the sounds of children shouting in the background.

"Hi, Claire. This is Harriet. Thanks again for dinner last night. It was lovely, and I really enjoyed getting to know your family better."

"We were so glad you could come. Although Bella hasn't given up on trying to get us to take her to Florida, so maybe I'm not so glad about that part."

"I'm sorry." Harriet laughed. "She would have fun though. Maybe you could go to a theme park here instead."

"Maybe someday," Claire said. "Anyway, what's up?"

"I'm not sure if you're the one to ask about this, but I was hoping I might be able to take a peek at some of the old church records," Harriet said. "I'm looking for information about a baptism."

"How old?"

"From the 1950s," Harriet said.

"That's hardly old at all. Sure thing."

"How far back do the records go?"

"Why, hundreds of years," Claire said. "Of course, the truly antique books are kept at the historical society in special humidity-controlled units, but something from the fifties would be at the church. I could let you in to take a look at those. When do you want to see them?"

"Whenever it's convenient. I don't want to put you out."

"You're doing no such thing. I'm happy to do it. How about now? I'm killing time at Desmond's football game anyway. I could pop over to the church and show you where the books are."

Harriet remembered the weather that morning. "He's playing soccer in the rain?"

Claire laughed. "It's barely a drizzle. If they didn't play in the rain, they'd never play around here. Meet in ten minutes?"

"That would be wonderful. I'll see you there."

Ten minutes later, Harriet parked in the lot behind White Church, a beautiful old Gothic-style building with a sharply pitched roof and tall stained glass windows. Harriet walked toward the section of the building that held the classrooms and offices. Claire's minivan was parked in the lot along with a few others, and Harriet found the back door unlocked.

She pushed open the door and stepped into a hallway lined with classrooms. A sign on the wall directed her to the church office at the end. Harriet found Claire seated at an oversized cherry desk in a room with high, pressed-tin ceilings, tall leaded windows topped with a round stained glass window of an angel, and an ornate fireplace mantel.

"Hello." Claire waved to her from the desk.

"This is some church office." Harriet was used to a sterile room tucked behind the choir robe storage at her church back home.

"It used to be a side chapel." Claire shrugged. "It's an old church."

"It's beautiful."

"It's not a bad place to work." She stood and gestured for Harriet to follow her. "Come on. The records are upstairs."

Harriet hadn't realized there was an upstairs, but she followed Claire out of the office and back down the hallway. As they passed one of the classrooms, they heard a scraping sound inside, and Claire stopped in the doorway. "Oh, it's you."

Harriet stopped beside her and peered in. Pastor Will Knight pushed a plastic chair along the linoleum floor toward a cabinet.

"Sorry to startle you, Claire. Hi, Harriet." Pastor Will gave them a wide smile. He gestured at a wooden cabinet against one wall. Cardboard boxes were piled on top of it in haphazard stacks. "I'm trying to find the sheep costumes from the Christmas pageant."

"You know it's only July, right?" Claire said.

"Is that right? So I should put back the Advent wreath too—is that what you're saying?"

Claire turned to Harriet. "Bet you didn't know your esteemed pastor is a wise guy."

"I don't believe anyone is under the delusion that I'm esteemed," Pastor Will said. "And I'm hoping to use a sheep costume for the children's lesson tomorrow, if I can find it."

"Ah. Well, in that case, Godspeed. I'm taking Harriet up to look at the old church record books."

"Good luck in the storage room. I fear that may be the one area of this church less organized than the Sunday school classrooms."

"At some point I'll take care of that, but for now we'll manage." Claire led Harriet down the hallway once more.

Pastor Will Knight wasn't married—Aunt Jinny had made sure to point that out to Harriet—but Harriet didn't know what his story was. She had a fleeting hope that she might get to know him a little better.

Claire refocused her by opening a door at the end of the hallway to reveal a staircase.

"Wow. I wouldn't have known this was here," Harriet said.

"It's an old building. It's got all kinds of nooks and crannies," Claire told her.

They climbed the stairs, which were hemmed in by walls covered in beadboard, up to an attic space with a high-sloped ceiling and more leaded glass windows. Claire flipped on the light, illuminating the space. The floor was a dark wood, and bookshelves and filing cabinets lined the walls. Boxes labeled CHRISTMAS LIGHTS and HOLIDAY BANNERS stood in one section, while another held old books. Piles of folding tables, communion supplies, and choir robes cluttered the floor. There was even an old spinet piano that looked to have seen better days.

"The record books are over here." Claire led Harriet to shelves stuffed with oversized leather-bound volumes. "You said you were looking for christenings in the 1950s?"

"That's right. Specifically, 1957."

Claire ran her hand over the spines of the books and pulled one out. "It should be in here." She laid the book on top of the spinet and opened the cover. She carefully thumbed through the thick pages, where names, dates, and other information was inscribed in ink.

"This is the section for baptisms, so it should be somewhere in here." Claire stepped aside so Harriet could stand in front of the book.

Harriet ran her finger down the list of names and dates, recognizing some of the surnames as families that still resided in the area. She flipped to the next page and ran through the listings from 1956 until she came to 1957.

There it was. *Liam Gregory Beresford, christened February 17, 1957. Parents Richard and Alexandra Beresford. Godparents Blake and Margaret Granger.*

Blake Granger was the man standing next to Richard Beresford in the photo. The one Liam resembled too strongly for it to be a coincidence.

Assuming she was right—and with the knowledge about Richard's blood type, Harriet was pretty sure she was—how had this been kept a secret for so long? Had no one noticed how much the little lord resembled his godfather instead of his supposed father?

More importantly, had Lord Beresford recently discovered that his biological father was not his actual father? Was that what had caused him to go tearing off to London at the drop of a hat?

Harriet tried to imagine the scenario. The truth must have come to light somehow. Maybe Peter had learned the truth—that he was actually the rightful heir to the Beresford title and house and fortune. That all his life, his older brother had been pampered and coddled, handed an estate and a title, while he, the younger brother, was forced to eke out his own living, all due to the circumstance of being born second. It would be enough to make anyone furious. She could understand why he might show up at the family's ancestral home and confront Liam—the false Lord Beresford—with the truth. It might be enough to make him threaten Liam or even injure him. To frighten Liam enough that he fled to London to—

To what? Head straight to the House of Lords, or whoever kept track of these things, and announce that his whole life was a lie? To show up at the house of his elder son and heir and let him know he would never be Lord Beresford after all, that one revelation had just changed the course of their lives? Or had he—

Harriet sucked in a breath. Or had he gone to London to silence the one person who knew the truth? If Liam's younger brother was the one who'd learned about his parentage, if he had shown up at Beresford Manor and threatened to reveal the secret, would Liam have tried to stop him? What might Liam have done to make sure the secret never came out? Had Gemma been right all along, that Liam had committed murder to keep his secret? Van had said there was no answer at Peter's door in London. Was that because he wasn't alive to answer the door?

Or had Liam gone to plead with Peter to keep his secret, but something else had happened between the brothers? Was there a legitimate reason Liam Beresford hadn't made it home to Yorkshire yet?

She was speculating—wildly. There was no proof of any of this. Still, the few facts she had all lined up with the new theory.

"Are you okay?" Claire watched her with concern.

"I think I need to talk to DC Worthington."

CHAPTER TWENTY-ONE

After Claire went back to the soccer field—or rather, the football pitch—Harriet drove to the police station and asked to speak with DC Worthington. DI McCormick was at her home station in Whitby today, but Van met with Harriet.

"I heard you did blood tests on the broken glass that was found in Lord Beresford's study," Harriet said.

"We did," Van said, suspicion clear in his tone.

"Let's say, hypothetically, that you discovered Liam's blood type was a certain type."

"Okay."

"And let's say, again hypothetically, that there were records around that recorded the blood type of Liam's father. Wouldn't it be something if you found out that they didn't line up?"

Van crossed his arms over his chest.

"Blood type is inherited. And certain blood types can only have children with certain blood types. And if you discovered that the baron's blood type and his father's were incompatible, that would raise some eyebrows, wouldn't it?"

"Do I want to know where you got this hypothetical information?"

"It's just a theory," Harriet admitted. "But if my theory is correct, it would be extremely unlikely that Richard Beresford was Liam's father, given their blood types. And then I found this photo." She showed him a photo she'd taken of the picture in the newspaper. "I realized that this guy looks a lot like Lord Beresford. That's Blake Granger, a family friend. I think, if we take the blood type seriously, that there's a chance he might be Liam's biological father. Which means—"

"One second. You're implying that Lord Beresford's father isn't the older Lord Beresford," Van said carefully. "That would be a really big deal, you understand? I don't know how much you know about how titles work here, but—"

"I know enough to know that it would mean he's not Lord Beresford," she finished for him. "That's what I'm trying to tell you. That would be a huge deal, right? The kind of thing worth, say, a scuffle in a study. Worth running off to London without telling anyone. Worth doing almost anything to keep the secret quiet. It wouldn't affect Liam alone. It would also affect his sons and grandsons. People will do crazy things to protect their family."

"You think Liam attacked or even murdered his brother because Peter had discovered that Richard Beresford wasn't really Liam's father?"

When he said it like that, it sounded impossible. But she had to press on, to get him to see the possibility she'd seen. "Or Liam might have hurt Peter, if he'd refused to step aside. You told me there was no answer at Peter's door. Maybe that's why."

"I suppose I can ask the London PD to go by again."

"Have they found Liam yet? We know he went to London, but has anyone seen him since?"

Instead of answering, Van replied, "I'll call the team down in London, and they'll go by to check on Peter."

"If he's dead, there won't be any answer. And if he did something to his brother, he's probably not hanging around his apartment waiting for the police to show up and ask him about it."

"Which will make his innocence quite clear when they find him at home," Van said.

He didn't believe her. Well, maybe she was mistaken. Maybe there was nothing wrong at all. Maybe Liam had gone to London on a spur-of-the-moment trip to see his brother, and they were having a nice time visiting and seeing shows in the West End and having tea at Claridge's Hotel and riding double-decker buses around to all the hot tourist spots.

Maybe.

But as much as Harriet wanted that to be the truth, she didn't think it was. "Will you let me know what the London police say?"

"I'll tell you what I can," he said. "It's an ongoing investigation, so I have to be careful."

"Of course."

She went through the grocery store on autopilot, grateful for her list, then headed home. When she pulled into the driveway, Aunt Jinny was in her garden, pruning roses. The drizzle had stopped, but the day remained cloudy, and the air felt wet.

"You look like you've got a bee in your bonnet," Aunt Jinny called. "Why don't you come talk it out?"

Harriet joined her aunt and told her about her trip to town—what she'd discovered in the library and at the church and what had happened in her meeting with Van.

"Blake Granger?" Aunt Jinny mused. "That's an interesting possibility."

"Do you know him?"

"No, the Granger family moved away before I was born," Aunt Jinny said. "I don't know why, but I got the sense when my parents talked about it that it was sudden, and kind of a big deal. They were very active in the community, but then they left and seemingly never came back. Dad might have known more about it, but I don't know what happened. Maybe it was simply a job situation or a family thing."

"Or maybe, as Liam grew, the resemblance became harder to ignore." Harriet showed her aunt the photo on her phone. "See? That's Blake Granger."

Aunt Jinny set her pruning shears down. "Oh my. Yes, that is hard to ignore. He sure does look like Liam Beresford. Or, rather, Liam looks like him."

"Maybe the Granger family moved away to prevent anyone from figuring out the truth," Harriet said.

"It would have been huge, the baron's lineage being questioned."

"The taxi driver said he drove a redheaded man to Beresford Manor last Friday. He was there long enough to fight with Liam before he had the driver take him back to the train station. I'd assumed it was Edward, but Peter also has red hair. What if he figured out the truth somehow and came here to insist that Liam step down and let him take over as the rightful heir?"

"That doesn't seem like Peter to me," Aunt Jinny said.

"How long has it been since you've spoken with Peter?"

"A couple of decades, I suppose."

"I know you were friends with him when you were younger, but people change. Someone can change a lot in a couple of decades," Harriet pointed out.

"They don't change enough to suddenly become murderers."

"Anything can happen in the heat of the moment if the stakes are high enough. Plus, we don't know that anyone is dead."

"I'm not saying I believe the possibility, but let's play this out," Aunt Jinny said. "So, you're suggesting Peter showed up at the house with the knowledge that his brother wasn't really the rightful heir. How might he have come by that information?"

"DNA tests these days are revealing all kinds of family secrets. Maybe that's what happened."

"Maybe. So, okay. Peter comes to the house, demanding that Liam step down, and when Liam refuses, Peter throws the decanter, runs off, and storms back to London." Aunt Jinny nodded as this version of events unfolded before Harriet's eyes. "Liam cuts himself on the decanter, likely while trying to clean it up."

"But then Liam couldn't leave the situation alone, not now that the secret was revealed," Harriet said. "He stood to lose everything, as did his son and grandson. So he went to London."

"And he confronted his brother," Aunt Jinny said.

"But Peter threatened to expose him, to seize what was rightfully his, when Liam refused to step aside."

"My goodness." Aunt Jinny shivered. "If it's true, that's quite a story."

"*If* it's true," Harriet said. "Van said he would ask the London police to check on Peter. I asked Van if he would report back, but he didn't seem to want to commit to that."

"So we won't know if it's true or not," Aunt Jinny said. "Not right away, anyway."

"I guess not," Harriet said. "I know I'm doing the right thing by continuing to share what I find with the police. I just wish I could see the results right away instead of having to wait until they're publicized—if they ever are."

Slowly, Aunt Jinny said, "Does it have to be that way?"

"What do you mean?"

"I mean, is there a reason we can't go to London ourselves?" Aunt Jinny asked. "It's not far by train. Or we could drive, which would be even quicker. But then you have to deal with parking, and gas is so expensive. I think we should stick with the train."

"Are you serious?"

"Why not? I've fancied a night in the city for a while now, and I don't believe you've been there since your move." Aunt Jinny spoke faster, clearly warming to the idea. "I have a friend in London. She has plenty of space, and she says I'm always welcome. We can stay the night with her. Maybe we could catch a show and eat a nice meal while we're at it."

"And have tea at Claridge's?" Harriet joked.

"Why not? Everyone should at least once."

Harriet gaped at her aunt. "Have you gone crazy? We can't simply run off to London."

"Why not?" Aunt Jinny asked. "I don't have anything else going on this weekend. If we leave soon, we'll get there with plenty of daylight left. How hard could Peter be to find?"

"I have his address," Harriet said, then immediately regretted encouraging her aunt's notion.

"So we go to his place and ask a few questions. Just to see what he says. And then we go enjoy London. Have you ever been to the bookshops on Charing Cross Road? There's a show at the Apollo that I want to see. I love London, and I don't make it there enough."

As crazy as she was acting, Harriet enjoyed seeing this side of her practical, levelheaded aunt. Still, she thought she should try to talk her out of it. "Aunt Jinny, we'd be interfering in a police investigation."

"Interfering how? By visiting an old friend?"

"You already said you haven't seen him in decades."

"All the more reason for us to catch up. Besides, we wouldn't be interfering any more than you already have, and I don't see anyone complaining about that. So far, you've found several clues for the police. Maybe you need to be the one to put the last puzzle piece into place."

"You're serious, aren't you?"

"Why not? At worst, we'll have a nice time with my friend and go to dinner and a show. At best, we'll solve a mystery while we're at it."

It was an insane plan. It was ludicrous to even think that they could show up in London and talk to Peter, let alone get him to confess to...what exactly? She wasn't even sure.

"What about Coleridge? And Charlie and Maxwell?" Harriet couldn't go gallivanting off to London at a moment's notice. She had responsibilities. That kind of thing was what had gotten them into this mess in the first place.

"I bet Polly could come by and feed them. What about Claire? I bet her kids would love to come over and play with the dogs until they're too tired to miss you. Or Doreen Danby would do it in a pinch."

Aunt Jinny was right. Harriet had already imposed on Claire enough today, and she didn't know her well enough to ask for more. But Polly would do it if Harriet asked. Doreen too.

But she couldn't simply go off to London. It would never work. It wasn't rational. It would probably get them in trouble with DI McCormick, and Harriet did not want to be in trouble with her.

But somehow, despite all that, she heard herself asking, "When's the next train?"

It turned out there were several trains that would get them to London from Whitby. If they hurried, they could make the next one. Harriet rushed home and tossed some clothes in her small suitcase. She packed a nice outfit in case they did go to a show on the West End, pinching herself to make sure she wasn't dreaming. But she was awake, and she was really facing that possibility.

She grabbed her passport, just in case—in case of what, she didn't know—as well as a phone charger, her laptop, and toiletries. A book for the train ride. She poured extra food into the dogs' and cat's bowls then called Polly, who agreed at once to help. She'd stop by tonight and tomorrow morning to take care of the animals.

Finally, Harriet hurried to meet Aunt Jinny, who was wheeling her suitcase to her car.

"Ready?" Aunt Jinny beamed as if this was some wonderful adventure. And Harriet supposed it was. When she'd woken up that morning, catching a train to London hadn't even crossed her mind. But now they were on their way, the countryside whipping past as they drove to Whitby.

They parked near the station and wheeled their suitcases into the lobby as a train from Scarborough arrived. Aunt Jinny scanned the board for the right train number. All around them, people streamed off the platform and into the station, wheeling bags, talking on phones, hugging loved ones in the lobby.

"There it is," Aunt Jinny said. "We have just enough time to buy the tickets."

She started toward the ticket machines, but Harriet's eye caught on something.

With all the people coming off the train and walking through the station, Harriet wasn't sure how she managed to spot them. Maybe it was the first man's red hair, or the fact that she had been studying the second man's face for a week.

"Aunt Jinny," she said faintly.

"Hang on. This machine doesn't make sense. We want two tickets to—"

Harriet grabbed her aunt's arm. "Aunt Jinny, *look*."

"What is it?"

In answer, Harriet pointed to where the two men strolled down the platform, wheeling bags and chatting. Laughing.

"Oh. I see now," Aunt Jinny said. "Oh my."

In that moment, Harriet understood what she was seeing and realized that she'd been so right and so wrong, all at once.

CHAPTER TWENTY-TWO

Harriet didn't know what to do, but Aunt Jinny didn't hesitate. She stepped forward and smiled as Peter and Liam Beresford walked through the station waiting area toward them. "Peter Beresford, is that you?"

"Jinny Bailey?" Peter's face broke out in a wide grin. "I can't believe it. You're as gorgeous as ever."

It really was Peter Beresford, alive and well. And the man next to him was unquestionably Liam. Lord Beresford. Who also wasn't dead. The baron held back a step behind his brother, and though his face didn't reveal much and his shoulders were stiff, he didn't seem unfriendly. He seemed reserved, in a very British way, plus a little shy.

"It's so good to see you." Aunt Jinny held out her hand for him to shake.

Peter stepped past her hand and pulled her in for a hug. "How are you? It's been forever."

"I'm well, thank you. It's good to see you." Aunt Jinny pulled away and made introductions. "This is my niece, Harriet. Arthur's daughter. She's come from the US to take over my late father's vet practice."

"It's good to meet you." Peter smiled at Harriet and shook her hand and then turned back to Aunt Jinny. "I'm so sorry to hear about your father. You remember my brother, Liam?"

"Lovely to see you again," Aunt Jinny said, nodding to Lord Beresford. "For so many reasons."

He held out his hand and shook Aunt Jinny's and then Harriet's. "Like what?"

"You don't know?" Aunt Jinny asked.

Liam shook his head, and Peter shrugged.

"You've created quite a stir, I'm afraid," Aunt Jinny told Liam. "The way you vanished, we all thought something horrible had happened. Everyone thinks you went missing. It's been in the papers and everything."

"Missing?" Liam narrowed his eyes. "Why would anyone think that?"

"Coleridge was found loose in the streets," Harriet said.

"He was?" The fear on his face made it clear he'd truly had no idea.

"He's safe," Harriet said. "Don't worry. Archie Osbourne brought him to my office, and I've been caring for him ever since."

"H-he's with you?" he stammered. "Archie Osbourne, the gardener? Oh my. Thank you." He frowned. "I wonder why—"

"Trey Casey was doing his best to care for him," Harriet explained. "But Coleridge got out while he was at work. And Mrs. Lewis didn't know where you'd gone. She said you never went anywhere, and you wouldn't have left without telling her. Plus, there was a mess in your study, and no one knew where you'd gone or if you were all right."

He opened his mouth and closed it again. "I didn't leave without telling Mrs. Lewis. I sent her an email explaining everything—why there was a mess in the study, what train I was taking, who was caring for Coleridge, and that I wasn't sure when I would be back."

"You did?" Harriet asked. "She didn't get it. I can tell you that. She was sure something terrible had happened to you." She gasped. "I remember now. Her computer isn't working. Her grandson spilled juice on it, and it's been in the shop."

"Oh dear. I should have called her instead. I thought it would be easier if she had the details in writing." Liam seemed chagrined.

"You've been quite the headline," Aunt Jinny said cheerfully. "A regular celebrity. Lord Beresford, missing. Perhaps dead."

"I had no idea," he spluttered. "I'm so sorry for all the fuss. I took the train to London. To see my brother. I didn't mean to get everyone in a tizzy."

"Yes, we can see that now," Aunt Jinny said, smiling. "And I'm glad you've made it back safely. Both of you."

"Though, actually, we should probably let the police know you're all right," Harriet said. "They've mounted a full search. The London police are on their way to your home now, Peter."

"They are?" His brow knitted. "Why in the world would they be?"

"It seems we have a lot to catch up on," Aunt Jinny said. "Harriet, why don't you call Van and let him know that Lord Beresford has been found, safe and sound."

A short while later, they were all seated in the great hall at Beresford Manor, cups of tea on the side tables and clutched in laps. Aunt Jinny and Harriet had driven the brothers to the manor house. DC Worthington and DI McCormick were on their way, but while they waited, Harriet explained why they all thought something terrible had happened to Lord Beresford and how they'd figured out what had really happened.

"I truly had no idea I caused such a fuss," Lord Beresford said. "I'm mortified."

"That's the last time my brother ever visits me in London," Peter joked.

"Everyone will be glad you're okay," Harriet assured the baron.

"What I can't understand is, why would you take your dog to a random person instead of boarding him with Harriet?" Aunt Jinny asked. "There are kennels on the property."

"I didn't have time to go all that way if I was going to make the train," Liam explained. "And Coleridge didn't know you, because I haven't needed to bring him to you yet. I figured I would only be gone a night or two, and the cottage was right there. I'd spoken to Trey several times, and he liked Coleridge. We often saw him out on walks. I went by, and he seemed willing. I thought Coleridge would be fine. Clearly, I had that wrong."

Harriet was surprised by the baron. She had expected someone with a title to be cold and aloof. Harsh, even. But Liam Beresford wasn't like that at all. He was reserved and measured, yes. He spoke quietly and didn't come across as warm or jolly. But he wasn't mean or off-putting. He'd insisted they call him Liam, forgoing the formal title. He seemed like a man completely overwhelmed by the strange circumstance he'd found himself in. He had welcomed Harriet and Aunt Jinny into his home to wait for the police to arrive and even served them tea while they explained to him all the things that had happened since he'd been gone.

Harriet told the brothers the different theories as to what had happened, from the coat that had made them think he'd fallen off the cliff—

"How grisly," Liam said, in the understated manner she was coming to realize was his typical way of speaking. "Mrs. Lewis donated that coat to a charity shop weeks ago."

"We figured that out eventually," Harriet said. "There was also speculation that you'd gone on a holiday to Spain."

Liam laughed at that. "Not likely."

"That's what Daisy Lyons said too."

"You spoke with Daisy?" Liam asked. Was it Harriet's imagination, or had his eyes brightened at the mention of her name?

"Between Harriet and the police, nearly everyone in Yorkshire has been interviewed about your disappearance," Aunt Jinny said.

Once again, Liam seemed at a loss for words. "But why? No offense, Dr. Bailey, but you don't even know me. Why would you spend time worrying where I went?"

Harriet sipped the rich tea from the delicate porcelain cup while she considered her answer. "At first, I was worried because of Coleridge. He was in my care, and I wanted to know when you were coming back. And then, when I tried to return him to you, Mrs. Lewis was so upset. She told me all the reasons she felt that your disappearance was suspicious. I naturally wanted to find out more, if only to assuage her fears. And you were friends with my grandfather, right?"

"Harold was one of my dearest friends," Liam said.

"Well, I'm living in my grandfather's home, and I took over his vet practice. I guess I thought he would have done the same. That he wouldn't rest until his friend came home for his dog. So I knew I couldn't either."

"You're so like him," Liam said. "I see him in your face when you smile."

Harriet felt herself blush, gratified by his words.

"Your grandfather was a great man," Liam said. "And he would have been proud of you. Thank you for all you've done."

Harriet felt tears well in her eyes, and she blinked them back. She missed Grandad every single day. But it felt good to be with people who also missed him.

"I still don't know what happened, why you left at the drop of a hat," Aunt Jinny said. Harriet tried not to laugh. It sounded as if her aunt was scolding the baron. "We figured out—well…" She coughed, and Harriet could see her trying to come up with a delicate way to say what they'd learned. "That is, we discovered some evidence to suggest that there might be some confusion about—"

"You learned about Blake Granger," Liam said, rescuing her.

"Yes," Harriet said. "We figured that part out."

"Well, you're quicker than I am," Liam said. "I've lived sixty-eight years without figuring it out. And the clues were there the whole time, if I'd bothered to look."

"But you wouldn't have thought to," Peter said. "None of us did. Why would we suspect that at all? Blake was a family friend, and after they moved away, we hardly gave them any thought at all."

"I wonder if he knew," Liam said. "Part of me wonders if that's why they moved away, to make it harder for anyone to make the connection."

"I don't know," Peter said. "It's hard to know, and the only people who could have told us are gone." He turned to Harriet and Aunt Jinny. "Here's what we've figured out. The Grangers and our parents were good friends, and they used to travel together sometimes. They went on a trip to Scotland together for New Year's the year Liam was born."

"We understand what happened," Aunt Jinny said.

"We don't know if Mum knew who my father was," Liam said. "But looking at photos now, it's pretty clear. Still, if she suspected, she never said."

"And why would she?" Peter asked. "If the truth came out, you'd lose everything. She didn't want that for you. Of course she kept quiet."

"I wouldn't have lost everything," Liam said. "I never really wanted all this." He waved his hand at the grandeur surrounding them. "I never asked for it. All it's brought me is misery these many years."

"No it hasn't, and you know it," Peter said, rolling his eyes. "You couldn't marry the woman you wanted, but you ended up with a fine wife and two wonderful sons."

"My children are the one good thing about this place. I'm grateful for them," Liam said. "But if it had been up to me, I would have stepped aside for you to take your rightful place decades ago. If I had known."

"There was a reason Mum never told," Peter said. "And I don't regret it at all. I never wanted this either."

"What do you mean?" Harriet took in the high coffered ceilings, the enormous paned windows, the delicate stonework on the mantel. She glanced at the fine rugs and draperies and the portraits on the walls and thought of the hundreds of years of family history it all represented. "Why wouldn't you want this?"

"It's a money pit, for one," Liam said bluntly. "It costs more to keep this house than the estate makes, and I'm responsible for paying the difference. It's unsustainable, and yet I'm tasked with sustaining it for future generations of the family."

"When you have several hundreds of years of Beresfords behind you, you can't simply decide to sell it," Peter added.

"That kind of legacy isn't discarded easily," Liam explained. "Besides, I'd be making that decision for all future generations. And how am I to know what they would want?"

"You know what one of them wants, anyway," Peter said.

Harriet couldn't read the look that passed between the brothers, but she understood that they had communicated something.

"I'm tied here, for another," Liam said. "Peter got to move to London, but I never could."

"But it's so lovely here." Harriet couldn't imagine any place she'd rather live than Yorkshire.

"It *is* lovely," Liam agreed. "But I love theater, architecture, and art. I love high-end food. London has all that. I would have liked the chance to make a name for myself, instead of inheriting the title that literally every firstborn male in the family has held for hundreds of years. I don't have my own identity. I'm simply one of the Baron Beresfords."

"I see your point, but making your own way isn't all it's cracked up to be either," Peter said.

"Which, I suppose, was Edward's point," Liam said ruefully.

"Edward knew?" Harriet asked.

"That's how this whole thing started," Liam said. "Edward's son, Robbie, did a project about DNA for his high school biology class. For extra credit, he could take a DNA test and build his family tree. Other members of the family had to take the tests for comparison purposes, so Edward and his wife took them, as did I."

"I took one as well, at Edward's request," Peter said. "I didn't see any reason to say no. I was happy to help my great-nephew with his project."

"But when the results came back, it was clear something was wrong straight away," Liam said. "Edward helped him enter it all in one of those genealogy sites. Peter's DNA didn't match Robbie's as closely as it should have. It looked as if Edward's side of the family came from a different place than Peter's. As if Peter and I had two different fathers." He took a sip of his tea, his hands shaking.

Harriet and Aunt Jinny waited for him to collect himself enough to continue.

"Well, these sites nowadays, they tell you about your DNA, but they also tell you who you're related to, based on your DNA. Peter was a close match for our cousins on the Beresford side, but I was not. After some digging, Eddie discovered that he and I had closer matches in the Granger family. So naturally he had some questions."

"That's one way to put it," Peter said.

"You have to understand," Liam said to Harriet. "If it was true, it meant that I wasn't the rightful heir to the Beresford title and lands. Which meant that Edward wasn't either. The law about this is very clear."

"I understand," Harriet assured him.

"At any rate, he came here last Friday."

Harriet had been right the first time. The taxi driver had brought Edward from the Whitby train station, not Peter.

"He showed up out of the blue with the DNA results, demanding to know what had happened and why his DNA didn't match his uncle Peter's. That was how I found out my father wasn't actually my father."

"Oh dear," Aunt Jinny murmured. "I'm so sorry. What a terrible way to discover something like that. Though I don't suppose there is a good way."

"I was shaken to my core. It took some time for the situation to sink in, and even more time for me to believe it, even though the evidence was right in front of me. But I finally convinced him that I really didn't know and it wasn't my doing. Then his focus shifted. He stopped berating me for keeping the secret from him and started telling me I couldn't ever let anyone know."

"He didn't want you to tell your brother?" Harriet asked.

"He wanted to rip up the results and never tell anyone. He knew what would happen if it came out. If I wasn't Lord Beresford, then he wouldn't be Lord Beresford, and that was who he'd been raised to be." He gestured around the room again. "This is the only future he'd ever imagined for himself. And if this went away, if he didn't inherit the lands and the title and money, he felt he had nothing."

"That's what the scene in the study was about," Harriet said.

Liam grimaced. "We had a difference of opinion. I said I couldn't keep this news from my brother. He said I had to, that I couldn't tell anyone. When I refused to do as he asked, he threw a decanter and stormed off. I cut myself trying to clean up the glass before I decided to leave it for Mrs. Lewis to take care of."

"Oh, Edward," Peter said.

"He's always had a bad temper, and his entire future was in my hands. It would have been upsetting for anyone."

Harriet considered the complicated emotions Liam must be feeling. For all his bad behavior and dubious motivations, Edward was still Liam's son. It was easy for Harriet to judge his behavior from the outside—it seemed like a temper tantrum from a rich boy who had learned he wouldn't be getting all the toys he thought he deserved.

But Harriet also realized that she couldn't understand the full weight of what was demanded of these families, of what hundreds of years of history and expectation meant for someone in the modern world. Maybe what appeared to be an entitled tantrum was more about the complications of trying to live out an ancient institution in the modern world, with all the layers of guilt and doubt and history that went along with it.

In any case, it wasn't her place to judge these men or their family or relationships. She didn't know what it was like. All she knew was that she still had questions.

"I know Edward left shortly after he arrived on Friday. But was it him you went to see in London the next day?" Harriet asked. "To patch things up?"

"No. He needed time to cool off," Liam said. "I went to see Peter. Once I knew the truth, I couldn't keep it quiet."

Peter laughed. "He showed up at my place, all serious, and told me he wasn't really the Lord Beresford—I was. But I'm not having any of it. He just wants to offload this place on me. As if I wouldn't figure that out." He grinned at his brother, clearly teasing him.

Liam shook his head. "He told me never to speak of it again. He refused to move to this 'gloomy old house in the middle of nowhere.' He doesn't want the title and never has. Apparently, if I tell anyone what I've learned, he'll disown me as a brother. I think that's a bit extreme."

"Not at all. I also said that I would spread lies about you to the press. I have no doubt they'll print anything I tell them," Peter added with a smile.

"So you want him to hush it all up and pretend you don't know the truth?" Aunt Jinny asked.

"Exactly," Peter said. "It might be the only thing my dear nephew Edward and I have ever agreed on. Neither of us wants this news to get out."

"I've been in London trying to change his mind ever since," Liam said.

"But the police said there was no one at your apartment," Harriet said.

"They must have come by while we were out," Peter said. "We didn't sit around the apartment debating, you know. It's London. There's so much to do. We went out."

"We saw several wonderful shows," Liam said. "I really liked the one playing at the Apollo."

"I'm hoping to see that one myself," Aunt Jinny said.

"Anyway, it eventually became clear that no matter how long I stayed, Peter wasn't going to change his mind. He's a stubborn old one."

"I don't care who your biological father was," Peter told him. "There's no reason to change things that none of us want changed. We'll keep this quiet and go on living our lives. You're still my brother, whether you like it or it. This is your life, whether you like it or not. If you don't like it, change it. Travel. Go ask Daisy to marry you after all these years. But don't mess up my life by telling everyone what no one needs to know. There's no reason to make trouble. To say nothing of what it would do to our mother's memory. She was a lovely woman who made an error in judgment that resulted in my amazing brother. I won't have her name dragged through the mud for that."

"That was the argument that swayed me," Liam said. "Peter decided to come home for a visit, and then he's going back to London and resuming his life. Now that you've showed up, demanding to know where I've been and saying everyone's looking for me, I guess I have to tell at least a few people what happened."

"Or come up with a good story." Peter motioned out the window. "And we'd better do it quickly. The police are pulling up now."

Harriet still had questions about what had happened and what the future would hold. She imagined this family had a lot to work through. But she was glad to see that they were both alive, in good spirits, and ready to do it together. Sitting in this ancestral home that had housed so many generations of Beresfords, she could almost feel the weight and importance of that history, and she was confident they would figure it out.

It reminded her, in some ways, of how she felt living in her grandfather's old home, running his practice. She didn't know if the interview she'd done with Gemma would ever be published, but Harriet realized what she'd told the reporter was true. Moving here, living here—it felt like coming home. Being surrounded by the places and people her father and grandfather had known, she felt the weight of her own family's history in Yorkshire, and it felt as if she had finally stepped into her place in it.

Harriet was musing on this feeling when there was a knock at the front door. Peter patted his brother's arm. "I'll go talk to them first," he said, pushing himself up. "That should give them a shock, if they think I'm dead."

Liam laughed, and Peter vanished toward the front hall. Then Liam faced Harriet with a serious expression. "Now. The most important question of all."

Harriet racked her brain, trying to think what it could be. Her mouth went dry.

"Where is my dog?" Liam said.

Harriet and Aunt Jinny laughed. When Harriet could speak again, she promised to return Coleridge that evening.

Suddenly, Harriet was sure that no matter what happened, they were going to be all right. The Beresfords would work things out, and every day she was here, White Church Bay felt a little more like home. She was settling in, making friends, and finding her place in this magical part of the world.

She couldn't wait to see what came next.

FROM THE AUTHOR

Dear Reader,

I was in college the first time I went to London. I was visiting a friend, and like most people who visit the UK, I fell in love. It was more than the double-decker buses and the scones and the accents, though all of those were pretty amazing. I loved the sense of history that pervaded the whole place. I loved walking the same streets that William Shakespeare walked, and seeing St. Paul's, which was designed by Christopher Wren three hundred years ago. I liked imagining what it all must have looked like in the time of Oliver Cromwell and William of Orange and Elizabeth I. Even the oldest buildings in the United States don't compare to the rich history found in this beautiful country. Of course, not all of English history is to be admired—that whole thing about colonizing half the world is generally recognized as a misstep now—but recognizing the mistakes we've made in the past and the damage we've caused is an important part of history as well.

I went back to visit my friend a few more times over the years, and together we explored many places, including Bath, which filled my Austen-loving heart, and Dublin, which isn't technically in Great Britain, but a short plane ride away in Ireland. But my favorite visit was the time we spent a night in an old manor house that was turned into a hotel in the Cotswolds. I loved the creaky floorboards, the mullioned windows, and the town pub that was several hundred years old. We played games in front of an enormous fireplace and pretended we were from another time. That manor-house-turned-hotel was the inspiration for Beresford Manor in this story.

I also loved that I got to center my story around a dog. I wrote most of this book while staying with my parents and their ridiculously cute labradoodle, Charlie. Shortly after I turned in the manuscript, my kids and husband finally convinced me to get a dog of our own—another labradoodle we named Sirius. Can I consider taking him for walks research for my next book? I also loved getting to know more about bloodhounds, which truly are an amazing breed. I learned they can track a scent trail more than 300 hours old and have been known to follow a trail for more than a hundred miles. In addition, bloodhound puppies are adorable.

I hope you enjoyed reading this book as much as I enjoyed writing it!

Signed,
Beth Adams

ABOUT THE AUTHOR

Beth Adams lives in Brooklyn, New York, with her husband and two daughters. When she's not writing, she's trying to find time to read mysteries.

A STROLL THROUGH
THE ENGLISH COUNTRYSIDE

Beresford Manor, home of Lord Beresford in this book, is fictional, but I based it on not only a manor-house-turned-hotel I once visited in the Cotswolds, but also on several other manor houses in Yorkshire, many of which are open to the public.

Castle Howard is one of the grandest, with 140,000 square feet of living space and 8,800 acres on the estate. This baroque-style manor was built by the 3rd Earl of Carlisle, who began work on the stunning estate in 1699. The manor has appeared in many films and TV shows, including *Brideshead Revisited* and *Bridgerton*.

Burton Agnes Hall, in the town of Burton Agnes, was built beginning in 1601, though the older Burton Agnes Manor House, built in 1173, is also on the property. The brick hall was designed by Robert Smythson, architect to Elizabeth I, and contains an impressive art collection and a walled garden.

Burton Constable Hall, just a short drive away, is another beautiful old home. The current house was built in 1560 and has been the home of the Constable family for over 400 years. It also has lush gardens and grounds, and a large art collection.

All of these houses, along with several others, are open to the public, and visitors can tour the homes and grounds. If you ever make it to Yorkshire, pop in and see how the landed gentry lived in another time—and how some of them continue to live today.

Aunt Jinny's Favorite Shortbread

Shortbread is easy to make, and so incredibly delicious. It goes perfectly with a cup of tea!

Ingredients:

1 cup (2 sticks) good-quality unsalted butter, room temperature

½ cup sugar

2 cups all-purpose flour

Directions:

Preheat oven to 325 degrees. In large bowl of electric mixer, cream butter and sugar until light and fluffy, about five minutes. Gradually beat in flour. Press dough into ungreased 9-inch square baking dish or pan, and prick top with fork. Bake until light brown, about 30 to 35 minutes. While shortbread is still warm, cut into squares or bars, and transfer to a rack to cool completely.

Read on for a sneak peek of another exciting book
in the Mysteries of Cobble Hill Farm series!

Into Thin Air

BY SANDRA ORCHARD

Harriet Bailey smiled at the sight of the young boy sitting in the waiting room of Cobble Hill Veterinary Clinic Friday morning, a docile hen roosting contentedly on his lap. "C'mon in, Allen. How is Rosie doing?"

The boy sprang to his feet. "Right as rain, Miss Harriet. She's mighty grateful for us saving her. She's laid a double-yolk egg every day since." He was referring to the practice of holding an egg up to a candle or other light source to see what was inside without cracking it.

Laughing, Harriet lifted the hen out of the boy's arms, being careful of its splinted leg. "Wow, that's high praise."

The boy grabbed an egg carton from the seat beside the one he'd vacated then followed Harriet to an exam room. "I brought you some. Not all Rosie's, since I wanted to give you a full dozen, but some of hers are in here."

"Thank you so much. I appreciate that."

Rosie pecked at Harriet's dangling ponytail.

Harriet deposited the inquisitive hen on the examination table then flicked her ponytail behind her shoulder and tucked the stray tendrils of dark brown hair behind her ears. "She certainly seems spry enough."

"She is. The other hens tried to peck at her splint, so I've kept her penned away from them, close to the house. And I visit her every day."

"I'm sure she loves all the attention." Chickens didn't always appreciate the ministrations of rambunctious young boys, but Harriet had witnessed Allen's extraordinary care and been impressed. She removed the splint from the bird's leg and examined it carefully.

Allen had raced over on his sister's bicycle a few weeks ago with the hen in the basket on the bike's handlebars. "I need to see the new lady vet," he'd blurted to Polly Thatcher at the reception desk. He said a fox had gotten into the hen's enclosure and injured Rosie before he could chase it away. To make matters worse, Rosie was his mother's favorite hen.

Harriet's heart warmed at the memory of the confidence the boy had placed in her capabilities. Several of the local farmers, especially the old-timers, were still wary of the idea of a *lady* vet— and an American at that—taking over her beloved grandfather's decades-old veterinary practice in the heart of North Yorkshire.

Harriet stroked Rosie's feathers. "I'm pleased with how her leg has mended. She shouldn't have any trouble with it now."

"I'm most grateful to you, Doc."

"It's been my pleasure."

He stuffed his hands deep into his jean pockets. "What do I owe you?"

Harriet glanced at the carton of eggs he'd set on her counter and knew exactly how her grandfather would respond. "Those farm-fresh eggs should cover it."

"Really?" He picked up Rosie and hugged her to his chest. "Oh, thank you! My dad said she weren't worth the brass it'd cost to mend her. But after she started laying double-yolkers, even he admitted she's a right grand hen."

Harriet chuckled. "I'm glad to hear it. She is indeed grand." She opened the door for him and gave a relieved sigh at the empty waiting room. After spending half the night seeing to a sick calf, she desperately needed coffee. As fond as she'd grown of the local's strong Yorkshire tea, she needed a bigger caffeine kick before facing the rest of the day.

As if she'd read her mind, Polly exchanged a mug of coffee for the carton of eggs Harriet held. The spunky twenty-four-year-old had been Harriet's grandfather's receptionist and assistant, and she'd happily stayed on to help when Harriet inherited his practice. She had also become a good friend.

"Do you have a date?" Harriet gestured to Polly's long dark hair, which had been hanging loose when Allen arrived with Rosie and was now styled in a casual updo. Harriet suspected a fair number of the young men who happened into the clinic with stray cats came in the hope of asking Polly out.

Polly fanned the loose tendrils still hanging about her neck. "No, just overheated. I pulled a couple of fans out of the supply cupboard, but they don't help much. I know it's August, but I can't remember it ever being this hot."

"Yeah, with Yorkshire being on the North Sea, I didn't expect to miss air-conditioning. It was never this hot when I visited Grandad in the summer as a kid. Even the beach was chilly."

Polly grimaced. "Until the last year or two, we never thought we'd need air-conditioning here. We considered hot weather a treat. And I know drinking hot coffee doesn't help, but you looked as if you needed one."

"I did. Thanks."

When Harriet's grandfather, Harold Bailey, passed away late last year, he'd left Cobble Hill Farm to Harriet, including the veterinary practice housed in the north end of the farm's two-hundred-year-old, two-story stone house where multiple generations of Baileys had been raised. The large property, surrounded by rolling dales dotted with sheep and cattle hemmed in by Yorkshire's iconic drystone walls, was about a mile north of the village of White Church Bay.

Still carrying the egg carton, Polly pushed through the door at the end of a short hallway behind the reception desk, which opened into the home kitchen. "I'm glad to see you at least got a dozen eggs out of Allen for your services this time." Her eyes twinkled with amusement when she glanced back over her shoulder.

Harriet trailed after her. "I couldn't very well have charged him for putting a splint on a chicken leg. Imagine what the farmers would have said about me. Besides, you know Grandad would have done the same thing." She'd gone through some of his records. Old Doc Bailey had frequently accepted barter in lieu of money for his services.

"For sure." Polly feigned a thick Yorkshire accent. "The lass put a splint on the bird's leg then made the lad pay more brass than he'd pay for a dressed chicken."

Harriet scarcely managed to swallow her swig of coffee without spurting it out on a laugh. "Exactly."

"Just wait," Polly warned, turning serious. "Once your soft spot for distressed youngsters gets out, our waiting room will be full of them with all manner of pets. And eggs won't pay the electricity bill, let alone the updates this place needs."

Snagging a cookie from the biscuit tin, Harriet groaned, all too aware that more than a few of her grandfather's once-regular farm clients had yet to avail themselves of her services. "I thought I struck a good deal with young Alfie when he offered to feed and water any animals in our care in exchange for insulin for his sister's cat."

"He's a good kid." It had certainly been a nice break for Harriet and Polly with more clients boarding their dogs during summer holidays, not to mention the donkey.

At the sound of Harriet fiddling with the biscuit tin, Maxwell clattered into the kitchen to mooch one, with Charlie not far behind. The dog and cat had come with the clinic. Maxwell was an adorable long-haired dachshund whose hind legs were paralyzed when he was hit by a car. Nevertheless, he happily motored around the place with a wheeled prosthesis that Harriet's grandfather had gotten for him.

Charlie had been rescued from a burning trash bin as a kitten. Her coat was patchy due to scars from the fire, but what there was of it bore soft-hued patches of gray, ginger, and white, which Harriet would call a muted calico. Harriet's grandfather had named all the clinic's adopted felines "Charlie" regardless of the cat's gender, claiming it was one less thing he had to remember.

Harriet treated Maxwell to a dog biscuit and Charlie to a fish-flavored cat treat. Maxwell practically inhaled his snack, but Charlie took her time examining the offering before she deigned to accept it from Harriet's fingers.

Polly helped herself to a cookie too. "At least the income from your grandfather's art gallery is helping make up for any shortfall."

Besides being a beloved country vet, Harriet's grandfather had become an accomplished painter of both animals and gorgeous scenes of the area's landscapes. He had opened the Bailey Art Gallery in the former carriage house on the property to showcase his work— a gallery that he had also bequeathed to Harriet, who had opened it up to visitors again last month.

"The write-up that blogger did on the discovery of the Henderson painting has boosted interest in the farm. Mrs. Winslow told me the number of visitors to the gallery has doubled and prints of Grandad's most popular paintings and other artsy souvenirs are flying off the shelves." Mrs. Ida Winslow had run the gallery since its opening and had graciously agreed to continue to manage it for Harriet.

"Yeah, and it isn't even going on display until next weekend." The blogger who'd offered to feature the gallery was Callum Henderson-Grainger, the grandson of the deceased farmer who'd left the painting to the gallery in his will. At first, Harriet had been worried Callum's request for a tour and interview was a ploy to convince her that the painting should remain in *his* family. The painting had, after all, been a gift from her grandfather to Callum's great-grandfather, long before Harold Bailey's paintings garnered national acclaim. But Callum hadn't so much as hinted that the painting stay in his family.

The gallery earned a reasonable amount from sales of souvenirs and Grandad's prints, and a donations box at the gallery entrance helped offset overhead costs, such as utilities and pest control and paying Mrs. Winslow to monitor the comings and goings of visitors.

Harriet swallowed the last of her coffee. "Do I have time to check in with the pest control guys before our next appointment?"

"You're done here for today. Unless an emergency call comes in, your afternoon is wide open."

"That's not a good sign." Not that a healthy pet population was a bad thing, if that was *all* that was keeping clients at home. "This makes two days in a row with no farm calls, not counting last night's emergency. Although yesterday's quiet schedule can be blamed on the Yorkshire Day celebrations."

"That's true enough."

Yorkshire residents were fiercely proud of their county's heritage and had been officially celebrating that fact on the first day of August for almost fifty years. Polly had even dragged Harriet to the town's local pub to hear the reading of "a declaration of the integrity of Yorkshire." She'd been fascinated to learn that the county's rich history could be traced back to the first millennium. In fact, the stone wall around the city of York had been standing for more than 1,100 years.

"I better go see how Ronnie and Rhys are doing." Harriet started out the clinic door that opened to the practice's parking area and almost bowled over a young woman carrying a ginger-haired, chubby-cheeked infant in a car seat. "I'm so sorry. I didn't see you there."

"No, it's my fault." The woman smoothed her hair. "I should have knocked."

Harriet held the door open and motioned her inside. When no pets followed, she asked the woman, "How may I help you?"

"We're here to see Dr. Garrett for my baby's eight-week checkup."

"I see." Harriet's aunt, Jinny Garrett, was the town's local physician. "Her office is in the dower cottage off the far end of the parking area."

Both homes sat well back from the road, so a client coming up the long driveway would first pass the carriage-house-turned-art-gallery on the right with the handful of parking spaces opposite it before reaching the larger parking area that served both Aunt Jinny's and the veterinary practices. Harriet's place stood on the right, and the dower house sat at a right angle to it at the end of the parking lot, with the entrance facing the road and the rear of the cottage offering a spectacular view of the North Sea.

A large meadow provided a buffer between the houses and the cliffside, and colorful, flower-filled gardens, like little sanctuaries, furnished green space between the buildings. Harriet especially appreciated the low stone wall around the property. A narrow lane perpendicular to the driveway ran past the gallery and around to the barn.

"I went to Dr. Garrett's first," the woman explained, "but the sign on her door said she was called to an emergency and won't be back for half an hour. I was hoping I might use your loo while I wait."

"Of course. It's right through there."

"You can leave the baby with us," Polly volunteered, clearing off a table to make room for the infant's car seat. "I wouldn't want you to put him on the floor with all the dogs and cats we get traipsing through here."

"I hadn't thought of that. Thank you." The woman set the car seat in the middle of the table. "Mummy will be right back," she whispered to the sleeping baby.

The moment she disappeared through the door, Polly let out a squeal. "Isn't he adorable?"

The baby's eyes popped open, and when they locked onto Polly, his bottom lip began to quiver.

"Oh, no. Don't cry, sweetheart." Polly unbuckled him. "Your mummy will be back before you know it."

"What are you doing?" Harriet asked.

"Taking him out before he starts crying." She lifted him to her shoulder, carefully supporting his head. "There, there. It's all right," Polly reassured in a singsong that could charm the most nervous feline.

Unfortunately, the baby didn't share their clients' temperaments. His whimpers turned to wails.

Polly bounced him gently, shushing him.

He didn't sound impressed.

"You know what they say," Harriet quipped. "Let sleeping dogs lie. I guess the same applies to babies."

"I can't understand it. The kids at the church's Bible camp love me."

"That's because you bring puppies and lambs to help tell your stories."

"You might be right." Polly lifted the infant off her shoulder and held him out to Harriet. "Here, you have a go."

Harriet cuddled the child and began humming a lullaby she remembered her mom singing to her when she was little.

He quieted immediately.

"Ah, you have the touch," Polly proclaimed.

Smiling, Harriet inhaled, savoring the sweet baby scent. If her fiancé hadn't broken off their engagement, they might have soon been welcoming a little bundle of joy like this into their lives. She swallowed the bitter taste that rose in her throat at how Dustin Stewart's rejection had not only ended their upcoming wedding and her dreams of starting a family but robbed her of a job too, since there'd been no way she could have continued to work in the same veterinary practice as him.

She gently swayed in rhythm as she continued to hum, reminding herself that she'd forgiven Dustin. After all, if he hadn't ended things, she might never have left Connecticut and traveled halfway around the world to Cobble Hill Farm to take over her grandfather's veterinary practice.

"I'm sorry, did he get fussy?" The woman's voice jolted Harriet from her thoughts.

"It's no problem. He's a lovely boy." Harriet carefully handed the content child to his mother. "You're welcome to wait here for Dr. Garrett if you like. We don't have air-conditioning, but it's a little cooler in here than outside."

"It's kind of you to offer, but there's a lovely breeze coming in off the bay. Now that Benji's awake, I can show him the neighbor's lambs."

"Mind you don't get too close to their alpacas. They like to spit," Polly cautioned.

The woman chuckled. "I'll remember that. Thank you."

Harriet turned to Polly. "I'm going to speak to the pest control guys. Feel free to close the office early today if you'd like. Just be sure to forward office calls to my cell phone."

"You got it."

Harriet waved to the young mother and hurried toward the art gallery.

Ronnie and Rhys of Reynolds Pest Removal Company were on ladders, removing ivy from the side of the building. The bare stone wall wasn't nearly as aesthetic as it had appeared when covered in lush greenery, but Ronnie had explained that they needed to remove everything that made it easy for the squirrels to climb to the roof and burrow in the attic. The destructive rodents had already caused enough damage. She was grateful she'd found a company that would remove them humanely. Gray squirrels were persona non grata, or rather *anima non grata* in Britain, since they'd driven the native red squirrel to the brink of extinction after being brought to the country in the 1800s.

"How goes the battle?" she called up to Ronnie.

The lanky man, who appeared closer in age to Polly's twenty-four years than Harriet's thirty-three, removed his tweed flat cap and clutched it to his chest as he met Harriet's gaze. "Those squirrels are right stubborn, and I'm fair *geffered* from the *mithering* task."

Harriet blinked, her mind whirling. *Geffered? Mithering?*

"But don't worry," he went on. "She'll be right by the time we're done. We'll catch all the rascals."

Don't worry, she mentally repeated, nodding. Despite having lived in the UK for months now, she still struggled to decipher what many of the locals said.

"Excuse me." A gray-haired man waved to Harriet from the pasture on the other side of the driveway. "Is this the Bailey Art Gallery?"

"It is indeed."

The man and his female companion wound their way through the turnstile, referred to by the locals as a kissing gate, that ensured farm animals didn't escape the pasture. Each day, at least a few visitors arrived at the farm via the public pathway that traversed the moors and linked up with the coast-to-coast trail along the cliffside. The pair hurried across the drive, walking sticks in each hand and sizable rucksacks on their backs.

Harriet pointed out the way then snagged her ringing phone. The office number appeared on the screen. "Polly, I thought I told you to take the rest of the day off."

"I was about to when an emergency call came in. Ned Staveley at Goose Beck Farm on Harbottom Road has a sick cow and needs you to come out. I'll text directions."

"Appreciate it. You can let him know I'm on my way." Harriet hurried to her vehicle, an ancient green Land Rover she'd not so affectionately dubbed "the Beast." She'd inherited it along with the practice. While climbing in, she saw the woman who had brought her baby into the clinic furtively duck into the trees.

But where was her baby?

A NOTE FROM THE EDITORS

We hope you enjoyed another exciting volume in the Mysteries of Cobble Hill Farm series, published by Guideposts. For over seventy-five years, Guideposts, a nonprofit organization, has been driven by a vision of a world filled with hope. We aspire to be the voice of a trusted friend, a friend who makes you feel more hopeful and connected.

By making a purchase from Guideposts, you join our community in touching millions of lives, inspiring them to believe that all things are possible through faith, hope, and prayer. Your continued support allows us to provide uplifting resources to those in need. Whether through our communities, websites, apps, or publications, we inspire our audiences, bring them together, and comfort, uplift, entertain, and guide them. Visit us at guideposts.org to learn more.

We would love to hear from you. Write us at Guideposts, P.O. Box 5815, Harlan, Iowa 51593 or call us at (800) 932-2145. Did you love *Hide and Seek*? Leave a review for this product on guideposts.org/shop. Your feedback helps others in our community find relevant products.

Find inspiration, find faith, find Guideposts.
Shop our best sellers and favorites at
guideposts.org/shop
Or scan the QR code to go directly to our Shop

**Loved Mysteries of Cobble Hill Farm? Check out
some other Guideposts mystery series!**

SECRETS FROM GRANDMA'S ATTIC

Life is recorded not only in decades or years, but in events and memories that form the fabric of our being. Follow Tracy Doyle, Amy Allen, and Robin Davisson, the granddaughters of the recently deceased centenarian, Pearl Allen, as they explore the treasures found in the attic of Grandma Pearl's Victorian home, nestled near the banks of the Mississippi in Canton, Missouri. Not only do Pearl's descendants uncover a long-buried mystery at every attic exploration, they also discover their grandmother's legacy of deep, abiding faith, which has shaped and guided their family through the years. These uncovered Secrets from Grandma's Attic reveal stories of faith, redemption, and second chances that capture your heart long after you turn the last page.

History Lost and Found
The Art of Deception
Testament to a Patriot
Buttoned Up
Pearl of Great Price
Hidden Riches

SAVANNAH SECRETS

Welcome to Savannah, Georgia, a picture-perfect Southern city known for its manicured parks, moss-covered oaks, and antebellum architecture. Walk down one of the cobblestone streets, and you'll come upon Magnolia Investigations. It is here where two friends have joined forces to unravel some of Savannah's deepest secrets. Tag along as clues are exposed, red herrings discarded, and thrilling surprises revealed. Find inspiration in the special bond between Meredith Bellefontaine and Julia Foley. Cheer the friends on as they listen to their hearts and rely on their faith to solve each new case that comes their way.

The Hidden Gate
A Fallen Petal
Double Trouble
Whispering Bells
Where Time Stood Still
The Weight of Years
Willful Transgressions
Season's Meetings
Southern Fried Secrets
The Greatest of These
Patterns of Deception

The Waving Girl
Beneath a Dragon Moon
Garden Variety Crimes
Meant for Good
A Bone to Pick
Honeybees & Legacies
True Grits
Sapphire Secret
Jingle Bell Heist
Buried Secrets
A Puzzle of Pearls
Facing the Facts
Resurrecting Trouble
Forever and a Day

MYSTERIES OF MARTHA'S VINEYARD

Priscilla Latham Grant has inherited a lighthouse! So with not much more than a strong will and a sore heart, the recent widow says goodbye to her lifelong Kansas home and heads to the quaint and historic island of Martha's Vineyard, Massachusetts. There, she comes face-to-face with adventures, which include her trusty canine friend, Jake, three delightful cousins she didn't know she had, and Gerald O'Bannon, a handsome Coast Guard captain—plus head-scratching mysteries that crop up with surprising regularity.

A Light in the Darkness
Like a Fish Out of Water
Adrift
Maiden of the Mist
Making Waves
Don't Rock the Boat
A Port in the Storm
Thicker Than Water
Swept Away
Bridge Over Troubled Waters
Smoke on the Water
Shifting Sands
Shark Bait

Seascape in Shadows
Storm Tide
Water Flows Uphill
Catch of the Day
Beyond the Sea
Wider Than an Ocean
Sheeps Passing in the Night
Sail Away Home
Waves of Doubt
Lifeline
Flotsam & Jetsam
Just Over the Horizon

Find more inspiring stories in these best-loved Guideposts fiction series!

Mysteries of Lancaster County

Follow the Classen sisters as they unravel clues and uncover hidden secrets in Mysteries of Lancaster County. As you get to know these women and their friends, you'll see how God brings each of them together for a fresh start in life.

Secrets of Wayfarers Inn

Retired schoolteachers find themselves owners of an old warehouse-turned-inn that is filled with hidden passages, buried secrets, and stunning surprises that will set them on a course to puzzling mysteries from the Underground Railroad.

Tearoom Mysteries Series

Mix one stately Victorian home, a charming lakeside town in Maine, and two adventurous cousins with a passion for tea and hospitality. Add a large scoop of intriguing mystery, and sprinkle generously with faith, family, and friends, and you have the recipe for *Tearoom Mysteries*.

Ordinary Women of the Bible

Richly imagined stories—based on facts from the Bible—have all the plot twists and suspense of a great mystery, while bringing you fascinating insights on what it was like to be a woman living in the ancient world.

To learn more about these books, visit Guideposts.org/Shop